PRAISE FOR *THE EMPOWER PROGRAM, K–2*

"One of the toughest jobs of teachers is maintaining a balance in the classroom. You understand they're just kids, but inevitably we all get frustrated like anyone else. We're only human. In Rachel Baker's work, we find a solution to that frustration problem. She writes in such a way that makes me feel like I can start doing this *tomorrow* and find success with her methods. Even more importantly, this offers an opportunity for every child—no matter their performance history—to succeed." —**Tracy Johnston**, Speech Language Therapist, Mantua Township Schools

"Camden Community Charter School has been implementing *The Empower Program, K–2* in every classroom. Our school has witnessed a decrease in behavioral issues and inappropriate outbursts through the use of the Vent, Rent, and Rebuild forms that children are able to use to think about their actions and get themselves back on track. Students have a voice through these forms and let us know when they don't feel safe or when they did not make safe choices. For students who are unable to write, pictures with words are used to help them express what they are going through.

Through this program our students have learned to make better choices when emotions are involved. The teachers have also learned from the lessons to monitor how they treat the children by their Tone of Voice, Facial Expressions, and Body Language. *The Empower Program, K–2* has improved the climate of Camden Community Charter School, and we really enjoy using a system that works for our students. I would recommend this program to any school that needs help with improving the climate of their school." —**Andrea Surratt**, Principal, Camden Community Charter School (Camden, NJ)

"As an occupational therapist working with children with multiple disabilities, I used *The Empower Program, K–2* on a daily basis. *The Empower Program* gave our students a way to understand the affects their actions have on others and gave our interdisciplinary teams a clear and consistent language to reinforce positive changes." —**Ryan Ahern**, MS OTR, P.G. Chambers School (Cedar Knolls, NJ)

"After using *The Empower Program, K–2* in two inner-city charter schools and in an Asperger's Social Skills Group, I found that the children have increased in their ability to use various social, problem-solving, and coping skills in a highly functional manner. They are able to appropriately and affectively communicate their thoughts and feelings about various social scenarios that occur throughout the day.

The children are becoming better advocates for themselves as they are becoming better communicators of their thoughts and feelings. They are also learning perspective taking as they learn to recognize the thoughts and feelings of others. In this program the children use problem solving skills to rebuild daily scenarios in order to learn and recognize better ways of approaching challenging daily events; while being taught to use appropriate social and coping skills to help them manage these events affectively." —**Nicole Pruett**, MS, DCC Outpatient Therapist and Behavioral Support Specialist, Camden and Atlantic City NJ School Districts

"*The Empower Program, K–2* serves as a vehicle to tap into students' socio-emotional and academic needs in the classroom setting on a dynamic level. It incorporates a kinesthetic experience with a modern-day twist that allows students of all differentiated levels to gain common ground in their learning. The program will serve as a reflection of progress for any school struggling with students who may need more than a simple academic tug and are seeking a positive classroom changing experience that encourages growth of personal skillsets and character." —**George Mankbadi**, Special Education Teacher, Paul Robeson Charter School (Trenton, NJ)

"I used Baker's *The Empower Program, K–2* in my second grade inclusion classroom and the results were incredible. Students were given a chance to take responsibility for their actions and found a sense of pride in the program's independent methods of correcting undesirable behaviors. The program not only gave students a chance to identify and change their behaviors, but created an environment in which they could develop and practice appropriate social skills together as a team. Students are now able to prevent behaviors from getting in the way of their learning and fun. I have watched my students make leaps and bounds in such a small period of time with *The Empower Program* and I am excited to see even more growth to come. I believe this program will work wonders in all types of school environments." —**Lindsay Siegman**, Special Education Teacher, Camden Community Charter School (Camden, NJ)

"What I loved the most about *The Empower Program, K–2* was seeing how quickly the students utilized the catchphrases "Rent," "Vent," and "Rebuild." It was heavily used in the classroom community." —**Regina Bell**, Behavior Intervention Coordinator/Anti-Bullying Specialist, Paul Robeson Charter School (Trenton, NJ)

"*The Empower Program, K–2* is a beneficial, organized social skills curriculum that allows all those that utilize it to infuse essential social skills into the classroom and in other aspects of the school. Because of its multi-sensory approach and scripted lesson plans, it makes it easy for all school staff members to deliver and implement the social skills, while also engaging the students. The depth and dynamic approach to the curriculum make it much more than just a positive behavioral support system." —**Brett Hoyt**, School Psychologist, Camden Community Charter School (Camden, NJ)

"*The Empower Program, K–2* social skills curriculum created by Baker has impressed me in several important ways. It is clearly built on a foundation of respect for students. The practices it teaches are developmentally appropriate. Throughout its processes, the importance of student choice and responsibility for self and others is emphasized. The techniques have proven successful in my personal observations of their use with students. Teachers recognize the wisdom and efficacy inherent in the design and find the program relatively easy to implement. As a result of the above, I have advocated its full implementation in both charter schools with which I work." —**Gaeton Zorzi**, Senior Vice-President for Elementary Programs Superintendent, CSMI, LLC, New Jersey Charter Schools

"As a member of the Culture Team, it is very easy to rely heavily on consequences when students present challenging behaviors. After working closely with Baker and being introduced to *The Empower Program, K–2*, I was able to create and implement various structures and supports for my students. The structures and supports that I was able to implement give students the tools and space they need to express themselves appropriately and respectfully. This has helped to create a more positive culture and has decreased the need for consequences such as suspensions and detentions." —**Brandon Millwood**, Director of Culture, Paul Robeson Charter School (Trenton, NJ)

"*The Empower Program, K–2* works for maintaining discipline while making the students feel empowered. It teaches our learners to have a sense of responsibility for the actions they choose while giving them the tools they need to make better choices." —**Khaleo Brown**, Student Support Officer, Camden Community Charter School (Camden, NJ)

"My second-grade students love *The Empower Program, K–2* because it gets them involved physically and keeps them actively engaged by letting them think, discuss, and practice acceptable responses when situations or other people make them upset. I would highly recommend it to anyone who wants to give students of all ages the tools to self-regulate and increase personal awareness and responsibility to make positive choices." —**Leslie Johnson**, Second Grade Teacher, Camden Community Charter School (Camden, NJ)

"I am currently working in a K–2 class with a mix of students. Several of my students were struggling with behavior and acting out a lot. I remembered Baker's program and realized I was getting mad at them for doing what they were not supposed to be doing, but was not explaining what they *should* be doing. I introduced pieces of *The Empower Program, K–2*. We reviewed a social skill a week, focusing on the ones my students needed immediately (*quiet hands, calm body, quiet tone*) then moved on to the others. I also set up a calm corner (a chair with a binder filled with all of the social skills). There are pictures for my nonverbal students, and they choose one of each picture. The teacher that assists the student or tells the student to go to the calm corner also assists in answering the questions.

I love how the program has given my students a voice when they forget what they should be doing. We also discuss all day making good choices, and how the right choices will give us good things (usually we play the Wii on those days).

One of my first graders is on the spectrum and struggles a lot with transitions. When we are transitioning from something he really enjoys, he becomes frustrated and lacks the words to state his feelings. At these times he may shriek and pinch the teacher who is announcing the transition. So one day I said it was time to transition. This child became upset and reached out to grab me, then instantly took a deep breathe, grabbed his own hand, looked down, took a deep breathe, and demonstrated the skills we review in the calm corner. All on his own. I was so happy to see this. He then whispered, one more turn." —**Joyce Marie Lewis**, Special Education Teacher K–2, P.G. Chambers School (Cedar Knolls, NJ)

The Empower Program, K–2

Concrete Strategies for Positive Behavioral Support

Rachel Baker

ROWMAN & LITTLEFIELD
Lanham • Boulder • New York • London

Published by Rowman & Littlefield
A wholly owned subsidiary of The Rowman & Littlefield Publishing Group, Inc.
4501 Forbes Boulevard, Suite 200, Lanham, Maryland 20706
www.rowman.com

Unit A, Whitacre Mews, 26-34 Stannary Street, London SE11 4AB

Library of Congress Cataloging-in-Publication Data

Names: Baker, Rachel, 1982–
Title: The Empower Program, K–2 : concrete strategies for positive behavioral
    support / Rachel Baker.
Description: Lanham, Maryland : Rowman & Littlefield, 2017.
Identifiers: LCCN 2016045397 (print) | LCCN 2016045685 (ebook) |
    ISBN 9781475827163 (pbk. : alk. paper) | ISBN 9781475827170 (electronic)
Subjects: LCSH: Affective education. | Social learning. | Early childhood education.
Classification: LCC LB1072 .B35 2017 (print) | LCC LB1072 (ebook) |
    DDC 370.15/34—dc23
LC record available at https://lccn.loc.gov/2016045397

Printed in the United States of America

Table of Contents

Foreword
   Dr. Anne Kendall Psychologist   vii

Acknowledgments   ix

Author's Note   xi

Introduction   1

Why Empower?   7

SECTION 1 – ENVIRONMENT   **13**

Environment Classroom Scenarios—"When this happens…."   15

Environment Research and Relevancy—"Why did that happen?"   17

Environment Concrete Strategies—"What can I do?"   23

SECTION 2 – ABILITY   **37**

Ability Classroom Scenarios—"When this happens…."   39

Ability Research and Relevancy—"Why did that happen?"   41

Ability Concrete Strategies—"What can I do?"   47

SECTION 3 – MOTIVATION   **55**

Motivation Classroom Scenarios—"When this happens…."   57

Motivation Research and Relevancy—"Why did that happen?"   61

Motivation Concrete Strategies—"What can I do?"   67

Appendix A: Environment P.O.P Resources   79
   Learn Your ABC's Glossary   80
   Correct and Connect Redirection Glossary   81

Executive Questioning Help Sheet   82
Rebuilding Area Making Suggestion Sheet   83
VENT Solution Sheet   84
RENT Solution Sheet   86
REBUILD Solution Sheet   87
RESPOND Solution Sheet   93

Appendix B: Ability P.O.P Resources   95
Common Language Prompts Sheet   96
Master Teacher Lesson Frame   98
Weekly Framework for Instructional
    Activities Grid   99
Student Social Skills Cards   100
Lesson Plan 1: Tone of Voice   107
Lesson Plan 2: Facial Expression   108
Lesson Plan 3: Body Position   109
Lesson Plan 4: Personal Space   110
Lesson Plan 5: Communication   111
Lesson Plan 6: Keeping Your Cool   112
Lesson Plan 7: Time and Place   113
Lesson Plan 8: Waiting   114
Lesson Plan 9: Asking for Attention   115
Lesson Plan 10: Listening   116
Lesson Plan 11: Handling Frustration   117
Lesson Plan 12: Communicating Frustration   118
Lesson Plan 13: Moving On   119
Lesson Plan 14: Accepting Consequences   120
Lesson Plan 15: Respectfully Disagreeing   121
Lesson Plan 16: Communicating Concerns   122
Lesson Plan 17: Joining a Group   123
Lesson Plan 18: Compromise   124
Lesson Plan 19: Problem Solving   125
Lesson Plan 20: Choosing Who Goes First   126
Lesson Plan 21: Identifying Goals   127
Lesson Plan 22: Breaking Down Big Goals   128
Lesson Plan 23: Strategies to Reach Your Goals   129
Lesson Plan 24: Strategies for Working in Groups   130
Lesson Plan 25: Finding Focus   131

Appendix C: Motivation P.O.P Resources   133
Quick Guide to Student Access Supports   134
SIMPLE Student Tracker   135
SCHEDULE Student Tracker   136
GOAL–REWARD Student Tracker   138

About the Author   141

Foreword

Rachel Baker has a passion for helping children. When confronted with teaching a group of unfocused and rowdy special needs boys, Rachel had to write her own playbook. Now she is sharing what she learned with us.

Rachel's kids are the kind of children that teachers often try to avoid because they are hard to manage. These are kids who in traditional schools are loud and disruptive or who retreat and avoid doing anything. These are kids who have physical disabilities, learning differences, emotional dysregulation. How do you motivate these children to give school a chance? How do you help them to get along with others? How to you help them feel that they are capable?

Imagine that you could get one of these challenging children to tell you what would work. Rachel does just that because she was one of these hard to teach kids. As a physically active girl with ADHD and dyslexia, she did not learn like others. Now having spent 14 years studying children through the focus of general education, special education and social work, she has come up with a short book that gives us the answers. Unlike many teaching guides, Rachel's program starts with stressing the need for an emotional connection with others in the classroom as the foundation on which all learning takes place. How can you bring a sense of play and adventure into school as a way of connecting with students? Rachel knows how to do it. I once watched Rachel come into a classroom of high school children referred by the courts for behavioral issues. One young man was ripping up paper and throwing it on the floor. Rachel challenged him to shoot baskets by throwing balls of paper into the waste paper basket. Suddenly the group of lethargic and tuned out students became animated and alive.

Rachel keeps it simple. She provides a clear and easy way for teachers to deal with the disruption common to all children. Instead of relying on authoritarian, punitive techniques, Rachel creates a classroom where children are the problem solvers. Are kids fighting over a pencil? What do the other children in the room feel might fix this? What does the pencil grabber think might work? Rachel argues that time spent up front respecting children and teaching them strategies to solve problems and help each other, will in the long run create a classroom that feels safe and caring, where real learning can take place.

Rachel helps children not only learn to solve problems, but also learn to read their own bodies and figure out what is going on inside. By using a safe retreat corner, children can learn to take time to identify what they are feeling. If they are frustrated, they can learn how to calm down. If they are discouraged, they can figure out what might help them feel better. Rachel explains how to help the child pay attention to the tone of his voice, his expression and his body posture as a clue to what is going on inside and a guide to how others might see him.

I have worked for thirty years as a child psychologist and understand how sensitive children are and how dug in they can get when they feel incompetent, unheard or unappreciated. Likewise I understand how many demands teachers and parents face, how overwhelming raising a child with differences can be. I have known Rachel throughout her life. As a child she was always a doer with great ideas and abundant energy. She has evolved into a thinker with dazzling insight into what makes children feel safe and appreciated, which in turn lets them plunge with excitement into their world. I got new ideas from this book and I bet you will as well. These ideas work not only with difficult children but also with calm, organized and eager children. In fact all children deserve this empowering environment and these effective teaching techniques.

Anne L. Kendall, Ph.D.
Co-author with Georgia DeGangi of *Effective Parenting Strategies for Hard-to-Manage Children.*

Acknowledgments

Thank you to my wonderful editor Sarah Jubar for giving me the opportunity to put my passion in print. Also thank you for your flexibility and understanding as the birth of my first daughter came just before the end of our journey to finish this book. I'm not sure many other editors would have been so supportive, understanding, and kind during such a hectic time.

Thank you to Dr. Anne Kendall for your stellar work in the field as well as your constant support. I feel very fortunate to be able to look to you for professional guidance and personal encouragement. I couldn't be more proud and grateful to have such an *altruistic, unique, nurturing,* and *talented* mentor to lean on! Thank you again and again!

Thank you to the Tookes family (Natasha, Ryan, Ryder, and Ryan L. Tookes) and also to Tierra Strothers for your amazing modeling skills! I have always felt so supported by all of you and to be able to have Ryder's incredibly handsome face be a part of a tool that other parents and teachers can use to empower their students and children feels like the perfect way to share that love with the world. Be ready Ryan L. Tookes, you're next!

Thank you to Ali Zeidan of Montclair State University for the surprise of your sudden acquaintance and even more surprising selflessness, time, and effort helping me consolidate research into usable, readable pieces. You are the truest form of karma that I have met and I am so privileged to be able to pay your gracious gesture of help forward to someone else down the road. Thank you again.

Thank you to Professor Carter, or "Brother Robb" for your wisdom, warmth, and spirit. You are so important to me and your support in helping me understand myself within everything I am writing along with your endless compassion for the frustration of that process is something I will always be grateful for. Thank you to Dr. Howard Stevenson for your immense work advocating for racial literacy and the lens in which you helped me to dig deeper into my own work. Thank you Professor Jack Lewis for your humor, humanity, and support. Finally, thank you to Eric Grimes for your honesty and willingness to make me face my own indecision. If it wasn't for that conversation we had about choosing to "create my own space" and the risks and rewards of such an action, this book might still have been just a repetitive rant instead of something I can now use to make the type of change I believe can exist. Thank you for challenging me to trust myself enough to follow through.

Also thank you to my fantastic former professors at La Salle University for providing me with such a solid foundation in advocating for quality educational environments for children by showing me what an inclusive, creative, and personal experience I could have as a college student myself. Thank you Dr. Greer Richardson, Dr. Frank Mosca, Dr. Carole Patrylo, Dr. Preston Feden, Dr. Robert Vogel, and Dr. Deborah Yost for your endless support.

Thank you to my fabulous group of Peer Reviewers: Tracy Johnston, Lorrie Weaver, Jenna Surmick, Lisa Edwards, Leslie Johnson, Thurayya Berry-Petteway, Melissa Triboletti, Elizabeth Kendall, Kristen Sigler, Adriane Henry, Dede Dede, Rashan Prailow, Keith Benson, Leah Z Owens, Kenya Hall, Alex Gomez, and Daniel Okonkwo. A special thank you to a peer reviewer by the name of Lutfi Sariamed for taking drastic measures to assure that I stayed true to finishing this book—whether that meant dropping by without notice to physically supervise my work sessions, providing daily, weekly, and hourly annoying phone calls or text messages to remind me to continue writing, or merely re-reading a section for the billionth time because I was desperate for more feedback at 2am. Thank you for being as crazy as I am.

Thank you to my dearest friend Kristen Sigler for always offering your understanding of my insanity, along with coffee, blunt feedback, and constant encouragement. Your pep talks reawaken my confidence and reignite my momentum. Thank you for making sure that the meat of what really matters got into this book. If it weren't for your feedback, that foundation may have gone missing. Also, thank you for your brilliant photography skills! Thank you for your light, your humor, and your zest for life.

Thank you to my mentor, coach, and friend Lorrie Weaver for always finding time in her insanely busy schedule to give me the most critical and thorough feedback imaginable. Your understanding of my "D-ness" along with my ADHD tendencies is not only what makes you such an amazing friend, but frankly, what also makes you such an incredible educator, coach, and professional mentor. You have the ability to hold the highest expectations while caring deeply and personally about children and families. I have always felt very fortunate to be able to grow from your guidance, encouragement, and support!

Of course, thank you to my amazing parents! I feel very fortunate to have grown up surrounded by the creativity, compassion, and encouragement that you both provided. Dad, while I wish I had more of your organization and brutal concentration skills, I will always be thankful that I can borrow your calmness and composure to help me when I feel frazzled. Mom, thank you for your energy, your understanding, and your unique sense of the world around you. Your vision of children, education, and people is what led me to want to become a teacher and what leads me everyday to consciously spread the type of "J.O.Y." you bring to my life. I love you both very much.

Thank you to my sister Sarah for being such an incredibly supportive, understanding, and calming influence during this whole process. As an astonishing author yourself, I have so much respect for your talent and feel grateful to be able to look to you for guidance and support when I need it. Your unique ability to break things down to what they really are and strip them of their intimidation, along with your patience has made every milestone that has occurred over the past two years of each of our lives not only possible, but also positive. Thank you for always being there.

Thank you to my husband, Shane Baker, for your continuous strength and support. When I told you I really wanted to take a leap of faith, change things up, and take time to make this book happen, you didn't blink an eye—you just smiled and said, "I have been thinking that all along." I can't imagine going through this process without your immeasurable patience, understanding, and love. Who else would help me unpack my laptop in the hospital to finish a manuscript mere hours before the birth of our first, beautiful baby daughter Nia Elizabeth Baker? I am so lucky and honored to have you as my husband, my partner, and my constant coach. I love you.

Finally and most importantly, thank you to my students. Thank you to my kiddos in Warren, Newark, Philly, Cedar Knolls, Trenton, and Camden for being my **most important teachers**. You are and always will be the reason I strive to help make school days better. Your charisma (Da'Quan), your talents (Zane), your humor (Ja'Quan), your ability to care for one another (Justine), your guts (Quameer), your good days and bad days (all of us), your ideas (Tahson), your personalities (Jessalyn), and most importantly, your ever growing sense of who it was that you were growing into has always made me realize who it was that I was growing into each day we were together. Each one of you is strong, unique, and important, and I hope you realize that you are the reason this book came to be. You were not only my inspiration, but now, the inspiration and reason for more students to have better days. Because after all, to quote Rahmir Sturdivant, "*Today is going to be a great day!*" Well done. I'm so proud of you all!

Author's Note

Rowman & Littlefield has made supplemental resources for *The Empower Program, K–2*, available as a single PDF formatted for easy and clear printing on 8.5" x 11" paper. These resources may be printed and reproduced in limited quantities for private use without obtaining written permission. To acquire a copy of the PDF version of these resources, please email **resourcematerial@rowman.com** with your request, providing both the title and author of the book*, The Empower Program, K–2: Concrete Strategies for Positive Behavioral Support* by Rachel Baker, along with proof of purchase.

Please share your experiences using the activities and handouts or any questions by joining the online community: www.empowerprogram.net, https://www.facebook.com/The-Empower-Program-356392857817970/, www.twitter.com/EmpowerPrgrm. You can contact the author via her website, www.empowerprogram.net.

Introduction

Do any of the following questions sound familiar?

- Feeling frustrated, burnt out, or overwhelmed by student behaviors?
- Spending a large chunk of your prep time writing incident reports?
- Feeling like you need to battle, babysit, or bribe certain students?
- Wondering why your curriculum isn't scripted for the behaviors you're seeing?
- Spending a large chunk of your after-school time making phone calls to parents?
- Feeling like you're doing so much but it's never enough?
- Wishing you could just get through the day, close your door and scream?

If you said yes to any or all of the above, then you have just confirmed that you are not a horrible teacher but, in fact, a normal human being reacting to a phenomenon similar to rush-hour traffic. We understand that it happens and it never completely shocks us, yet it always seems to ruin our day. When negative student behavior seems like an endless groundhogs day of bumper-to-bumper traffic with no end in sight, both you and your students stop thinking about ways to navigate and tend to just pull over, get out, and shut down.

Now imagine . . .

- Feeling confident, refreshed, and ready to actually teach
- Spending a large chunk of your prep time drinking hot coffee or maybe prepping?
- Wondering why your curriculum is feeling more like a tool than an obstacle
- Spending a large chunk of your after school time . . . after . . . school . . . having . . . time
- Feeling like you're doing so much, you're connected to your students and it's actually working!
- Spending time calling parents to report positive outcomes

With this book, I offer you the modern day luxury of a "behavioral GPS." This book affords you options to breathe when you would previously hyperventilate, outlets of understanding where you have formerly felt blind, and real strategies that prepare you to be positive and productive each day—even when "traffic" occurs.

The tools in this book will:

1. Provide you with concrete strategies
2. Reduce your stress
3. Empower *all* of your students to feel safe, successful, and connected

GOAL #1: PROVIDE CONCRETE STRATEGIES

My first goal is to support you, the educator, with concrete strategies that allow you to support your students with compassion and sanity. With eleven years of teaching experience, I have been in your shoes many times before. Having also served as a social worker, outpatient therapist, parent advocate, behavior specialist, director of special education, and youth organizer, I can tell you that prioritizing the social–emotional development of our students is as important as promoting their academic achievement. I can also understand that this sentiment feels extremely *unhelpful* when it is simply stated and not followed by an action plan. In fact, when talking with teachers, most tell me they feel extremely overwhelmed and entirely under prepared for this double-responsibility.

How many times have you heard these educational buzzwords, "Positive Behavior Interventions and Supports" (PBIS), "Response to Intervention" (RTI), or "Social–Emotional Learning" (SEL)? Have you ever wondered why none of those acronyms seem to spell "Help Educators Learn Practical Meaningful Explanations" or (HELP ME)? Perhaps these buzzwords become so frustrating because you are rarely shown *how* to actually do the wonderful things they seem to stand for. Imagine all of those buzzwords like an old bin of cheap crayons that have broken into a million, tiny, seemingly unusable pieces. This book takes those pieces, boils them down, cools them off, and reforms them into several sturdy new crayons that you can use to spell FINALLY!

Therefore, I will deliver tangible resources that are realistic for you to implement and practical for your students to use. In this book you will find strategies and plans that you will actually have time to use even if you feel constrained by large class sizes, required curriculums, and/or minimal prep time. This book is not going to explain some antagonistically simple philosophy behind behavioral support; it is instead going to respect you, consider your real-time classroom frustrations, and give you the practical steps you have been asking for that make buzzwords like "behavior management" . . . well . . . *manageable*.

How will I do this, you may wonder? With

- Concrete tools such as forms, checklists, and charts in the appendix of each section
- Real examples of strategies in use and word-for-word models that can be used easily
- Plans and activities that are flexible for the time you have and your experience level

GOAL #2: REDUCE TEACHER STRESS

My next goal is to reduce your stress by not only giving you easy-to-implement methods for making student situations less sticky, but also by giving you genuine ways to build enduring relationships with your students that stick. Remember the traffic analogy? Anyone who has commuted through a high traffic area knows the pain of having to travel a very short distance on your odometer, going about two miles an hour with your blood pressure soaring through the roof. However, if you have ever stumbled upon a back road to travel, which may read *slightly* longer on your odometer, but you can travel 35 miles an hour without having your cardiologist on speed dial . . . that sounds like a much better option!

I use this second traffic comparison to assure you that while learning to build more positive, trusting relationships with your students may *feel* like something that takes longer or feels out of your way—given everything else you have to do—the result is the same as finding an alternate route to work. You will feel less stress getting up for work, enjoy your ride, and arrive in a totally different mindset than you had when you just had to grin and bear the daily grind.

All educators recognize the awkward balancing act between managing student behaviors and simultaneously trying to cultivate compassionate relationships. Over-managing student behavior can create a relationship that feels tense, while under-managing student behavior can leave you feeling out of control. Regardless, you're often left with the same hair-pulling question: How can I empower rather than overpower my students, while still keeping a controlled classroom?

The strategies in this book have been tested and proven, not only by teachers across school settings, but by me on my most stressed day with kids feeling the same stress. I can tell you first-hand that the most stress relieving "behavior management" trick I have ever learned was not something I was taught at all. It was the composite result of a long and multi-role career, making mistakes, going back, reflecting, and finding out that ultimately, the relationships I built with students in the most un-tricky of ways was the answer. This book will reveal the magic behind that trick in a far faster way for you.

GOAL #3: EMPOWER STUDENTS

My final goal is to empower *all students* to feel **safe**, **successful**, and **connected** in their educational environment. I emphasize *all students* because this program has worked for both general education students as well as students with learning, behavioral, or emotional needs. Despite how complicated it can sometimes feel, it is possible to implement strategies that both narrowly focus support using specific behavioral interventions for your most challenging students, and have those same strategies benefit the rest of your class in a positive way. While this "buy one, get one free" scenario may seem too good to be true, or worse, may even sound eerily like the rhetoric I swore against, I assure you I will make it real!

To prove it, I have organized this book into three sections that give you direct ways to address each of those three student goals. To put it simply, teachers get support—students get supported!

3 Sections for 3 Student Goals

Section 1: Environment—Safe

- You get a space to refresh your emotional mindset—students get a refreshed teacher
- You get explicit help using positive verbal redirection—students get positive help
- You get tangible tools to enact positive behavioral support—students get supported

Section 2: Ability—Successful

- You get social skills to teach—students get to learn how to navigate social situations
- You get activities reinforcing those skills—students become engaged and use them
- You get easy-to-follow plans—students get a teacher with time to engage them

Section 3: Motivation—Connected

- You get ways to give responsive behavioral feedback—students get less reactive
- You get visual, interactive methods to track behavioral progress—students progress
- You get guides for offering choice and leadership—students get to choose and lead

Who Should Read This Book?

Any and all educators should read this book. When I say "educators," I am referring to those people who inhabit the important yet vulnerable space of supporting children through their learning process. This includes, but is not limited to, teachers, parents, coaches, therapists, paraprofessionals, social workers, mentors, after-school program coordinators, and school administrators.

HOW IS THIS BOOK ORGANIZED?

Inside Each Section

Each of the three sections outlined will be broken down into three parts:

1. Classroom Scenarios—"When this happens . . . "
2. Research and Relevancy—"Why did that happen?"
3. Concrete Strategies—"What can I do?"

Classroom Scenarios

To introduce the section, I will narrate a typical scenario that you may be noticing in your classroom. That scenario (version 1) will then become the base for a second scenario (version 2) depicting the same circumstances only this time applying strategies that provide positive behavioral support. These vignettes will allow you to relive the frustration of certain behavioral situations while also feeling the immediate gratification of an alternate scenario with a much happier ending. The best news, however, is that I will then help you engineer the same ending in your classroom using a new set of strategies.

Research and Relevancy

The *Research* segment will allow you to pause briefly before getting right into the strategies, for that much antici-pated stress relief I promised! By reading the small pieces of solid research I explain here, you will be able to *know* the reasons behind what your students often *show* in those classroom scenarios.

The *Relevancy* segment will continue to support your capacity to build trusting relationships with your students, by presenting a "bigger picture" perspective. This perspective will contextualize the student behaviors you may be seeing within a wider social and cultural lens. Instead of merely highlighting the statistical struggle, the facts in this segment are presented in order to empower you to take an active role as an agent of change.

For example, I will present the realities of race and disability on disproportionate disciplinary treatment for stu-dents. I will then use those same educational statistics to inspire rather than discourage your active role in chang-ing those outcomes. I will present the negative side effects of ignoring such relevant factors, while simultaneously pointing you in the direction of how to use the information I have provided to make practical steps forward.

Concrete Strategies

The final *Concrete Strategies* segment of each section will then explain each strategy. I will use both experiential analogies and step-by-step instructions allowing you to navigate this book according to the time you have and learning style you prefer. These strategies will be followed up with *"P.O.P"* or *"Point of Performance" Resources*. These are tangible, take-away resources such as ready-to-use charts, checklists, forms, guides, student skill cards, and lesson plans that will be conveniently located in a specific appendix for each section.

Each *"P.O.P Resources Appendix"* functions like the best suitcase you have ever owned. It packs up all the key information from each section in a neat and orderly way so that when you need to unpack those strategies, they roll out smoothly. The *P.O.P Resources* in each appendix allow the strategies to work *for you*, as opposed to being yet another thing you *have to do*.

There are also directions at the end of each section for where to find additional online resources for support. These resources include "strategies in action" video footage showcasing the strategies being used inside real class-rooms, downloadable posters, additional reproducible worksheets and interactive blog support!

Key Points Shadowboxes

As another way to honor your time as busy teachers, you will find "Key Points" shadowboxes throughout the text. These will provide you with quick reference summaries of each section as you read in the *extremely unlikely* event that you are short on time. I believe the word you are looking for is "Pa-HA!"

TO SUM UP

This book will give you a sigh of relief at the end of your once disillusioned sticker chart, knowing that this time your reward is, in fact, real. My ultimate goal is to support you as you continue to engage in the critical work of creating educational spaces that support students. The positive effect you can choose to have on your students now may not only equip them with the skills they need to succeed in school, but can reach even further, empowering them to sustain that success *personally* as a transforming factor in their lives beyond the classroom.

Why Empower?

CREATE AN EXPERIENCE

The following activity is interactive, so be ready! Right now take out two pieces of paper and something to write with. On the first piece of paper, please write down things that you love to do and are really good at. Write down talents, interests, hobbies, and especially things that make you feel unique. On the second piece of paper, write down the mistakes you have made today, this week, or this month—both big and small. Now choose the mistake you make the most frequently and circle it.

Imagine that someone else wrote the mistake you circled on a label with a bright red marker and stuck that label to the middle of your chest. Everywhere you went, the first thing that people would notice was this bad habit of yours, written clearly on your chest like a warning. Certain people might even look at you and wonder when you would make that mistake next. How would you feel walking around with this new accessory? Take a moment to write down a few comments about your feelings on the sheet with your mistakes written on it.

Now, please take the piece of paper with all of the things that you are great at, fold it up into a really small square, and put it on the highest shelf that you can find. Imagine going through your day following the rule that, if it's written on that piece of paper hidden on the shelf, you cannot use it. How would the rest of your day play out? How would you feel navigating your day without your sense of humor or favorite piece of technology handy? Would you look at work differently if you couldn't use your wit to get a friend to smile, take time on your lunch break to talk casually with a peer, text message your spouse, or use your smart phone to check sports scores and breaking news?

How would you feel putting your best assets or unique interests on a shelf until the end of the day? Perhaps right now you're wondering what all of this imaginary paper folding has to do with the social–emotional education of your students.

ANALYZE THE EXPERIENCE

The first piece of paper symbolizes all of the fabulous, empowering, confidence-preserving qualities that your students possess. The second piece of paper represents your students' mistakes and misbehaviors. Unfortunately, in the daily grind of school, we can sometimes forget all of the positive and powerful information on that first piece of paper that allows students to feel a sense of belonging and value in our classrooms.

This usually happens because the one or two constant mistakes or misbehaviors those students present start to feel like a big fat label that seems to be stuck on their chest. The more they misbehave, the more we label them as "the bad kids." This cycle can cause us to put all of their positive qualities on a mental shelf and forget that those qualities are the very instruments that best reignite their positive behavior.

The strategies presented in this book will allow you to focus on your students' assets instead of feeling overwhelmed by their missteps. We will walk through concrete ways to build your classroom **environment**, empower your students with positive behavioral **abilities**, and provide constant **motivation** to ensure that your students always have access to that first piece of paper with those wonderful, empowering assets that will fortify every academic task they embark on. Welcome to a renewed and refreshing shift in focus from negative behaviors to positive opportunities!

Key Points

The inadvertent "label" we sometimes put on frequently misbehaving students can have a negative effect on the students' self-perception and derail our goal of redirecting and empowering their positive behavior. By shifting our attention from negative assumptions to positive assets, we can both empower students while also promoting pro-social behaviors.

THE BIG PICTURE

Why did you become an educator? What goals did you hope to make possible for your students? Take a moment to write a few thoughts down now on a sheet of paper. Now, think of some reasons why getting to that destination might be tough for you or your students. Perhaps learning differences, resources, student misbehavior, language barriers or cultural disconnects came across your mind? The million-dollar question remains, what do *all* students have in common, regardless of their differences? Give up?

all DRIVEN by

feelings or emotions

The answer is simple: they are all driven by feelings or emotions. Think of these feeling or emotions as the fuel that drives our thoughts and actions. Later, you will have a chance to read some chunks of research behind this interplay of emotions and actions, however, for now, let's examine this relationship by sitting in the driver's seat.

If we think about emotions as the fuel that drives our actions, imagine that fuel driving you in one of two distinct directions: positive and productive or negative and destructive. You might be asking yourself, "Well what happens when I don't feel any emotion at all?" At that point, your lack of feeling will either drive you to create a stable, neutral action like being able to remain seated or remain working on a task (positive), or create inaction, for example lacking the motivation to start a task at all or the unwillingness to change an existing non-productive behavior (negative).

but which direction?

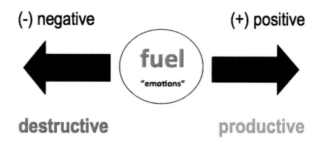

This process is the same for our students. When they enter our classrooms each day, their feelings and emotions drive them in either a positive or negative direction. Those feelings then create productive or destructive behaviors that affect the general learning environment of your classroom.

The purpose of *The Empower Program* is to provide students avenues, highways, and entrance ramps for positive behaviors while illuminating detours, side roads and exit ramps for negative behaviors. When we consider our goal as teachers, most think about advancing academic achievement, which is understandable. I would add to that goal that students also learn to identify themselves as positive, empowered, and autonomous members of society. The academic achievement we strive to engage means very little when students do not feel worthy or independent as true owners of that knowledge. The good news is we can do both! We can teach towards academic excellence while also fostering individuals who care about others as well as feel proud of themselves.

Key Points

All students come into our classrooms with feelings and emotions that drive their behavior in either a positive or negative direction. This book will provide concrete ways that enable students to choose a positive direction for their behavior.

The Concept of "Reclaiming"

Have you ever felt unacknowledged, overlooked, or disregarded? Unfortunately all children, and all people for that matter, have felt devalued at some point. What usually helps you to overcome this negative, sometimes even mentally debilitating feeling?

An excellent answer to this question has been developed and elegantly translated through the work of *Larry K. Brentro, Martin Brokenleg & Steve Van Bockern* in their incredibly powerful book *Reclaiming Youth At Risk.* The following research is taken directly from their text and was my inspiration for providing teachers a way to implement concrete social–emotional learning instruction through a "reclaiming" environment.

Brentro, Brokenleg and Bockern explain the concept of "reclaiming" as follows: "The reclaiming environment is one that creates changes that meet the needs of both the young person and the society. To reclaim is to recover and redeem, to restore value to something that has been devalued."

They go on to detail the features of the reclaiming environment:

- Experiencing **belonging in a supportive community** rather than being lost in a depersonalized bureaucracy.
- Meeting one's **needs for mastery**, rather than enduring inflexible systems designed for the convenience of adults.
- Involving youth in **determining their own future**, while recognizing society's need to control harmful behavior.
- Expecting **youth to be caregivers**, not just helpless recipients overly dependent on the care of adults. (p. 4, *Reclaiming Youth At Risk)*

The Circle of Courage

All of this work draws from the Native American concept of "The Circle of Courage." This circle represents the four qualities that must be present to raise a child that is both confident and compassionate. Each of the four qualities play an equal role and must be considered during child rearing in the Native American culture.

These four quadrants represent four qualities that create the perfect lens from which to view an environment that supports positive child development. This circle also provides a helpful frame from which to apply the strategies you will learn in order to create a concrete path towards that child's positive development.

For each section, the relevancy segment will connect back to a specific quadrant within "The Circle of Courage." The skills and strategies within each section will then demonstrate how to make these seemingly ethereal concepts practical.

THE CRUX OF IT ALL

Create an Experiment

This activity is one that demonstrates the importance of social–emotional learning in the larger scope of school planning. Feel free to get these materials and take part in this activity yourself, or simply just read through the explanation (but what fun would that be?)

You will need index cards, paper clips, a pen or pencil, popsicle sticks, scraps of paper, or cardboard and straws. The directions are simple. You are going to engineer a tower. You are only allowed to utilize the materials listed above. Your tower must fulfill the criteria below.

1. Your tower must be at least 12 inches tall (please measure exactly)
2. Your tower must be at least 4 inches wide (please measure exactly)
3. You must write what you want your students to learn in your classroom this year somewhere visibly on your tower

Were you able to construct a tower? Did the tower meet all of the criteria listed on the card? Do you feel satisfied with your work? Now, please test the strength of your tower. If you have access to a blow dryer, set the blow dryer on high and aim it right for your tower. What happened?

If your tower blew down, what would have helped it stay up? *(if your tower didn't blow down . . . play along and think about what would have helped if it had blown down.)* What would have helped your tower to withstand the high winds of the blow dryer? What about shaving cream?

Imagine (or actually go ahead and do this) recreating the same tower using lots and lots of shaving cream as a foundation, stucco, a binding agent, or whatever you think will fortify your tower. Now try the blow-dryer test again. What was the result?

Analyzing the Experiment

In response to this experiment, a phenomenal early childhood educator Elizabeth Kendall once said, "The fluff is the stuff that makes kids tough!" This quote perfectly summarizes the purpose for this shaving cream experiment—to make ridiculously concrete the role that Social–Emotional Learning plays in our classrooms!

In our experiment, the school supplies represent the academic side of what happens in the classroom. The rules that I gave you represent the state standards and curriculum you must teach with. The shaving cream, however, represents the less often considered social–emotional aspect of your teaching.

The shaving cream represents the social–emotional skills that have the potential to fortify our students learning by giving them the ability to withstand the stress of school while they are trying to withstand the stress of learning. As teachers, you diligently engineer lesson plans every day in order to provide the best possible academic instruction for your students. Knowing this, why would you possibly spend all of that time and energy on planning only to have it all fall down when the winds of stress blow through?

The impact that social–emotional learning can have on the strength and resilience of your students is the same as that of the shaving cream in our experiment. It holds in place all of the academic skills that you are trying to teach. To put it into another context, how many times have you planned amazing lessons, but students were not mentally available for learning? For instance, have you ever been half way through a lesson when negative student behaviors cause students to be removed from your classroom? This common occurrence begs the question: If your teaching is great, but students aren't mentally available or even present to receive it, how effective can you possibly be?

This example is particularly important when we think of the incredibly gifted students that become sidetracked by violence in their communities, struggles at home or trauma in their lives that no one can see coming. The once "frivolous" concept of social–emotional learning becomes much more important when you consider it as a necessary intervention that provides a foundation for students desperately in need of positive emotional reinforcement and stability amidst these difficult circumstances.

Simultaneously, the same social–emotional learning skills that provide reinforcement also act as extension opportunities for students to prepare for jobs requiring these twenty-first-century skills. Having the confidence to navigate responsible decision-making, build social awareness and practice positive relationship skills will serve to insulate their trajectory towards success well after they have left your classroom.

Key Points

The "Crux of it All" is Social–Emotional Learning. This acquired skill is not only important to our students' education, but the necessary binding agent that is often times missing. Examples of students who are innately very intelligent but consistently face violence in their communities, struggles at home or trauma in their lives present another significant need for social–emotional learning. Therefore, incorporating social–emotional learning into your educational planning, such as using the skills and strategies that follow in each section, will not only support the academic learning within your classroom, but will also prepare students to lead more confident and empowered lives outside of school.

SECTION 1

ENVIRONMENT

ENVIRONMENT CLASSROOM SCENARIOS

WHEN THIS HAPPENS . . .

Aiden and Jessica – Version 1

Midway through the second sentence of your read aloud, a voice to the right of you screams, "Hey! Stop doing that!" As you turn your head, you see Aiden flicking his pencil back and forth, touching his desk, then another student's desk, then his, and then back to hers.

"Jessica, please don't call out, okay?" you say, and then turning to the boy holding his pencil, you make a reasonable request: "Aiden, stop doing that, please."

You quickly continue reading. As you begin to start your next sentence, you hear laughing from Aiden's direction. When you look over, you see that he has put the pencil in his ear now instead of tapping it on his desk. His friends nearby begin to laugh along with him, and you struggle to stay calm.

"Aiden!" you command, "get that pencil out of your ear immediately!"

Aiden continues to laugh as he takes the pencil out of his ear and rolls it along Jessica's desk instead. As you feel your blood begin to boil, Jessica chimes in yelling, "Look, look he's doing it again!"

You respond annoyed, "Jessica, I can see that. Aiden, give me the pencil. Now."

You walk over to Aiden, take the pencil from his desk, and tell him to sit up and fold his hands in front of him. Aiden crosses his arms and turns his face away in a huff. You think to yourself, at least that's over, now where was I with this lesson? No sooner do you turn your head when you hear, "Heeyyyyyy. . . . stooopp itt!!!!!"

Jessica is now desperately pointing her finger at Aiden. "He stuck his tongue out at me. I saw him!" You purse your lips together and sharply exhale through your nostrils.

"Aiden, I am going to have to call your mother after school today. This is unacceptable."

As you walk back from his desk, you see two more students having a side conversation and redirect them by saying, "Do I have some other students who need a phone call home as well?"

You feel like you must regain control of your classroom.

When they stop, you say, "Now where was I . . . " and another student begins to answer. You seem to involuntarily snap back. "Raise your hand!" The student stops and seems upset, but you move on with the lesson, hoping you can get through the next 5 minutes without an interruption.

WHAT IF THIS HAPPENED, INSTEAD?

Aiden and Jessica – Version 2

Midway through the second sentence of your read aloud a voice to the right of you screams, "Hey! Stop doing that!" As you turn your head, you see Aiden flicking his pencil back and forth, touching his desk, then another student's desk, then his, and then back to hers.

You pause from reading and look to the whole class.

"Hmm, let me stop and think. I wonder if someone can raise their hand and suggest a way that Jessica could respond instead of reacting? I think we know a couple of really good strategies Jessica can use because she seems to have a pretty good reason to be upset."

You call on an eager student on the other side of the room who answers, "She could ask him to stop nicely?"

"Excellent thought, Leo. Anyone else have an idea, maybe a social skill? Yes, Janelle?"

"She could ask to communicate with Aiden?" Janelle suggests.

"Really good, Janelle. I like that one, too."

You turn back to Jessica and silently offer up both hands.

Jessica turns to Aiden and says, "Aiden, I don't like it when you touch my desk. Can you please stop?"

You gesture to the rest of the class to wiggle their fingers towards her as a sign of group praise as she waits for Aiden's response.

Aiden grumbles, "Sorry . . . "

You deliver a cheesy wink and say, "Thanks for respecting Jessica's concern, Aiden. Now, instead of tapping that pencil of yours on Jessica's desk, can you point it up here at my book and tell me where I was? This old lady lost track!"

Aiden giggles and points to the sentence you were reading.

"Pheww, thanks. Okay, everyone give a wink when all my listeners have their pencils securely fastened in their desks!"

You gaze at each student, silently nodding to recognize compliance. You clear your throat and continue to read.

ENVIRONMENT RESEARCH AND RELEVANCY

WHY DID THAT HAPPEN?

The Research

What did Jessica, Aiden, and you—the teacher—all have in common in the first scenario? Each of your actions was driven by your reaction to stress. Since one goal of this book is to reduce teacher stress, read the following explanation of *why* this happened by learning how both your brain and the brains of your students produced these reactions. When you know *why* and *how* something happens, you can begin to feel more in control of *what* you can do to change it.

It's time to get in the metaphorical driver's seat again and navigate this classroom stress. Let's start by using a car as our main example. Let's say you know nothing about car mechanics. When your car begins to make any sound related to a potential mechanical issue, you become immediately stressed out. This stress comes from realizing that there is a clear problem with one of the parts of your car and you have absolutely no idea how to fix it.

Your friend, however, is an auto mechanic by trade. When he hears the same sound, he experiences very little stress. He knows how each part of the car works together, can determine where the problem is coming from and employ several ways of fixing it. That sense of calm is what you can finally feel as a teacher by taking these small pieces of research and connecting them with concrete classroom strategies. This will allow you to feel more like a mechanic than a maniac when problems occur in your classroom.

Key Points

The goal of this research and relevancy section is to show how stress relates to student brain function and identify strategies to help manage that interaction.

The Limbic System – THE ENGINE

Let's begin by looking at the parts of your brain that produce the stress response or "the engine" of the problem we were seeing in both scenarios. Have you ever been walking through the park, felt something slither against the back of your leg, and jumped up screaming? Why did you choose to do that? The answer is that you didn't *choose* to do anything. Your instantaneous reaction was caused by a series of involuntary chemical interactions in an area of your brain known as the Limbic System.

Your Limbic System is a complex series of neurons that form a network in the brain that, among other things, inform your emotional responses. One of these sets of neurons is called the amygdala, sometimes referred to as the "fear center" of the brain. When a threatening stimulus is presented, your amygdala immediately processes that stimulus and triggers a fear response.

When this happens, your sympathetic nervous system shifts into overdrive causing your heart to beat faster, your blood pressure to rise and your senses to become more alert. Your body then releases adrenaline to your muscles in order to prepare for a potential fight or flight response. Isn't that being kind of overdramatic when it was really just an extra thick blade of grass that brushed up against the back of your leg?

The key to understanding the stress response initiated by the amygdala is that it is immediately triggered whether the threat is real or imagined. This is important to remember considering that this means absolutely no real "thinking" occurs during this process. Your primal instinct for survival causes your brain to go into "auto pilot" first. It is only *after* you have escaped, avoided, or faced the assumed threat that your brain even considers "thinking."

When we say "thinking," we're talking about a secondary step where an area of your brain called the thalamus processes information and sends a signal to the cortex enabling us to become conscious of what we actually heard, saw or felt. In short, whether we like it or not, our students (and we as teachers) **feel before we think!**

When we consider this primary feeling response as "the engine" then we can better understand how our students' engines work. Since we cannot change the fact that our students come in with ample fuel in their engines, we can now at least understand where that fuel is being used and why we sometimes hear those engines revving up.

The Power of Prosody – THE JACK

This concept of feeling before we think can become as useful as having a jack vs. having a pair of chopsticks to work with when your car gets a flat tire. Understanding that emotional reactions supersede conscious thoughts allows us to see that while we cannot always prevent what triggers a child's emotional response, we can learn to come prepared with tools that will help. Knowing that you have a triple-A card, a mechanic friend just a phone call away, or at the very least a car jack means that you can relax knowing the situation will be improving soon.

On the other hand, when you don't have these tools, you often further provoke your stress response and make the situation worse. Imagine having to try and jack up a car with a pair of chopsticks? In a classroom context, using negative or emotionally charged correction tactics with students can cause more stress and be less productive, much like trying to use chopsticks to jack up a car.

Research on the concept of prosody is one example of a simple yet effective tool. Prosody is defined as the emotional side of language. We process language in the right hemisphere of our brain where we can interpret things like pitch, inflection, rhythm, and tone. Understanding that we feel before we think, consider what happens when a friend uses sarcasm under his breath about something that you are taking seriously. Consider what happens when your boss raises her voice at you in front of your peers. What happens in your brain?

For students, the reaction is much the same when a teacher's tone of voice sounds hostile. To preface this, it is important to emphasize that sometimes you may have very valid reasons for *feeling* hostile in response to that student's behaviors. This is understandable given the stress that you yourself are feeling. Many teachers say that they feel they can only be effective when they present with a loud voice, as they feel this commands control. There is a difference, however, between a strong tone and a hostile tone. The point is, however frustrated you may feel, remember that the tone you use as a result may only serve to make matters worse instead of better for both yourself and the student you wish to redirect.

If we lift up the hood, so to speak, you will remember that the limbic system processes a "hostile tone" stimulus as a threat, even though you may not rationally process your own voice as a *real* threat to the child. When this occurs, the "auto pilot" fear response is activated which in turn, prevents the cortex or "thinking" part of the child's brain to get a word in edge wise. This can then translate into the child's "fight" response, which we know can present in many other colorful ways. This can also cause the child to present a "flight" response where they completely disconnect or shut down.

Now, let's visualize this happening. In reaction to a stressful misbehavior, you yell or snap your voice quickly, for example, to redirect the child. What do you want to happen? You probably just want the student to stop the negative behavior and start "thinking." But let's now go back under the hood and look at the mechanics of what's happening for the child during this verbal exchange.

As the tone of your voice begins to sound aggressive, the child's brain begins to dump all of its energy into fighting back, escaping, or shutting down. As teachers, all we want is for our students to use their "thinking" brain instead of continuing to engage in negative behavior. Using the car analogy, as much as you may want the chopsticks to act as a jack, chopsticks are simply not the most effective tools for the job. Thus, understanding how your students react to your prosody will allow you to monitor your use of prosody most effectively to redirect them.

Remember, this can be extremely difficult when you are under constant stress! That being said, understanding that your students' feelings of stress are just as valid and real can actually help prosody work for, rather than against you.

The Hormones of Stress – THE GAS or THE BREAKS

The final drivers in this demolition derby of chaos you are beginning to feel may be described as hormones. Researchers have utilized SPECT (Single Photon Emission Computed Tomography) scans to reveal an increase in the release of the hormones cortisol and adrenaline when the brain is under stress. Think of *cortisol* sounding a lot like the word and concept of *alcohol* for adults. Alcohol can sometimes cause adults to ramp up their behaviors and lower their ability to inhibit the same way that cortisol lowers a child's ability to inhibit behavioral responses when they are stressed.

Now, let's think of adrenaline as "the gas." Visualize that same child now increasing the speed at which their thoughts are running around their own brain knocking over stop signs left and right. Even more frustrating, when the stress response dies down what's known as the "adrenaline dump" takes place. This means that, having just cycled through this fear response, the child becomes mentally drained and has trouble refocusing on what to do next. As you may have guessed, the SPECT scans also revealed a visible decrease in working memory at this very same time.

So what about "the breaks?" There has to be some hope for control in this scenario, right? Yes, there is because the same SPECT scans also reveal that when a child is not stressed, there is an increase of activity in their prefrontal lobe, or their "thinking brain." Consequently, there is also an increase in the level of the hormone dopamine. This hormone allows for a feeling of relaxation, which aids in the ability to think more clearly. We can think of the hormone dopamine as "the breaks."

Stressful situations are bound to exist in our classrooms and our students' brains come factory-made with engines ready to drive off a cliff in the other direction or shut down altogether. This sounds terrifying—but fear not. The strategies that follow will provide some easy to access roadside assistance. Each strategy will focus on a way to use what you have just learned to allow your students to find their breaks, provide you with multiple jacks for an assortment of flat or blown out tires and most importantly, allow you to engage your students' engines to drive in the direction of learning.

Key Points

The Limbic System—THE ENGINE —We feel *before* we think

- The Limbic System is a complex series of neurons that inform emotional response
- The amygdala works alongside as "the fear center" causing "fight or flight" responses
- The Cortex (responsible for cognitive thought) is a *secondary step* after the limbic system

Prosody—THE JACK—Tone can be a *tool* or a *weapon*

- Prosody is defined as the emotional side of language
- Students respond to a hostile teacher tone much like the "fight or flight" response
- Understanding how to use tone in a positive, productive manner is essential

> **The Hormones of Stress—THE GAS and THE BREAKS—*How* stress affects thinking**
>
> - When under stress, the brain increases its release of the hormones cortisol and adrenaline. Cortisol lessens the ability to inhibit. Adrenaline speeds things up. Less working memory.
> - When NOT under stress, the brain increases its release of dopamine and activity in the prefrontal cortex. The prefrontal cortex allows for cognition while dopamine allows for a more relaxed state. This increases thinking and working memory as a result.

The Relevancy

Shifting from research to relevancy, the "big picture" connection here links to the concept of *Belonging*, the first quadrant in the "Circle of Courage."

When we show that we value a sense of belonging in our classroom, our students feel emotionally safe. This sense of emotional safety can lower their anxiety and decrease their need to behave in reactive or defensive ways. When students feel like they belong and are valued, this also increases their availability for learning and investment in their classroom environment!

On the other hand, when this sense of belonging is missing in the classroom, students can present as guarded, unattached or isolated. A need for belonging can also cause students to more easily succumb to peer pressure and become misled due to their incredible need to find a way to feel emotionally safe.

Relevancy in a Cultural Context

Data

- *"African-American students and those with particular educational disabilities were disproportionately likely to be removed from the classroom for disciplinary reasons"* (Breaking Schools' Rules: A Statewide Study on How School Discipline Relates to Students' Success and Juvenile Justice Involvement, 2011).
- *"African American over-representation in exclusionary school discipline cannot be explained by poverty status or differential rates of behavior. As a result of the "punitive and exclusionary discipline," these students have an increased risk of other negative outcomes"* (Race and Social Problems: Restructuring Inequality, 2015).
- *"Minority overrepresentation in school punishment is by no means a new finding in school discipline research. Investigations of a variety of school punishments over the past 25 years have consistently found evidence of socioeconomic and racial disproportionality in the administration of school discipline"* (The Color of Discipline, 2002).
- *"Studies of school suspension have consistently documented the overrepresentation of low-socioeconomic status (SES) students in disciplinary consequences. Students who receive free school lunch are at increased risk for school suspension (Skiba et al., 1997; Wu et al., 1982). Wu et al. (1982) also found that students whose fathers did not have a full-time job were significantly more likely to be suspended than students whose fathers were employed full time." Also, in a study conducted by Brantlinger (1991) "both low- and high-income adolescents agreed that low-income students were unfairly targeted by school disciplinary sanctions," per the student interviews. For instance, "while high-income students more often reported receiving mild and moderate consequences (e.g., teacher reprimand, seat reassignment), low-income students reported receiving more severe consequences, sometimes delivered in a less-than-professional manner (e.g., yelled at in front of class, made to stand in hall all day, search of personal belongings)"* (The Color of Discipline, 2002).

Questions

When you read the above information, what thoughts come to your mind? How might these facts affect the empowering classroom environment that you, as a teacher, aim to create? Have you ever felt conflicted when reading about these realities and then wondering how you can change them for your students? How can you, on a personal level, relate to these findings? What do you feel after you read them again?

The Good News . . .

These statistics highlight the reality of the impact the environment of your classroom, your emotional mindset as a teacher, and your knowledge of disproportionately unequal consequences can create for your students. These facts are not here to deter or discourage you. Instead, they are being presented to remind you of the extensive reach and great power that you, a single teacher, possess to change these outcomes for your students. Both individually and as a collective, the students facing this differential treatment are not only in need of teachers who take these facts seriously, but sitting inside of your classroom at the crossroads of injustice and opportunity each time you consider using them to inform the way in which you teach.

By simply taking a moment to remind yourself of the disproportionate trends that have existed and continue to exist for students of color and those with disabilities, you are taking one step closer to changing those trends for your students. The second and most crucial step is to employ the strategies in the sections that follow not only to provide your students with the important sense of belonging we spoke about earlier, but also to chip away at the cultural and racial inequities that have existed in education and discipline for far too long.

These strategies were written for *all* students, in order to improve their chances of experiencing an educational environment with less punitive discipline and more positive methods for identifying themselves as meaningful members who belong in your classroom community. If all students could walk into classrooms where teachers like you had concrete tools to foster their sense of belonging, **all** students would benefit.

ENVIRONMENT CONCRETE STRATEGIES

WHAT CAN I DO?

After realizing how much you *can't* control about a child's brain, now let's focus on what you *can* control. Below are five strategies that will help you to feel less stressed and more in control of establishing a safe and positive classroom-learning environment.

These strategies are broken down into three different types: foundation, verbal, and structural.

1. The *foundation strategies* are a compilation of quick tips for building trust with your students. They range from simple actions to more creative strategies, but all have been tested and approved by the most critical of student minds.
2. The next two strategies are *verbal strategies* that allow you to use what you just learned about prosody to inform verbal cueing in response to student conflict.
3. The final two strategies are *structural strategies* that incorporate tangible tools such as pre-made worksheets and specially designed areas of your classroom that prepare you to proactively manage behavioral conflicts.

The wonderful thing about these strategies is that, with a small amount of initial planning, you will be able to feel much more prepared even for the types of student reactions you can't see coming. Instead of panicking when a negative behavior arises, you will already have what you need to help your students and yourself. No daily anxiety required!

FOUNDATION STRATEGIES

Strategy 1: Build Trust

This concept seems obvious, but is never really discussed in practice. It's usually a well-intended sentiment that is stated at the beginning of the year during professional development, but rarely operationalized, exemplified, or explained. Below are eleven tips for building genuine trust with students that can function as both the glue and foundation for all of the other empowering strategies in this book. Without trust, your teaching is merely an exchange of information from one vendor to another, independent of one another except for the walls around you. If your students don't want to buy it, there's nothing you can do about it. When you choose to spend time building trust with your students, your teaching develops into a symbiotic relationship *with* your students and that changes the game entirely.

When reading this section, remember that, just like anything long term, building trust requires time and consistency. Knowing this, give yourself a break and don't try and conquer every one on day one! Allow yourself to use these tips for what they are, a foundation to build upon, not rush through or pile on top of everything else you have to do. With that being said, take a deep breath, relax and enjoy this glimpse into some helpful and tested trust-building tips!

Tip 1. Give J.O.Y

A fabulous early childhood educator by the name Elizabeth Kendall coined this expression and it is key to all of the following foundation strategies. "J.O.Y" stands for "Just Offer Yourself." This strategy may seem simple, but the range of its influence is staggering. *Just Offering Yourself* means allowing your students to get to know you as a person as opposed to just an educator. Though this concept can feel abstract, below are some concrete ways to do it:

- Share personal stories about your life, your goals, and your dreams
- Tell your students about your family and involve them in family moments you can share
- Share your personal interests, hobbies, and talents
- Allow them to ask you questions about your feelings and be truthful in your response
- Involve them in your struggles and ask them for their opinions and advice
- Show them you're a part of their classroom community by using words like "we" and "us" instead of "you" and "I"
- Be there—try to keep multitasking to a minimum if a student needs you to listen
- Talk about them behind their back . . . by proudly reporting back when you brag to others about their personalities and achievements outside of the classroom
- Invite people into your classroom that are important to you. Sharing their time and making those connections proves to your students that *they* are important to you!

Tip 2. Cultivate Caregivers

Students come into school in a perceived role—receivers of care. One of the most genuine ways to show pride, investment and trust in your students is to allow them to become caregivers as much as receivers. Try offering your students these options:

- Ask your students for advice . . . and thank them when you use it
- Allow your students to help you in small ways that matter (reminding you of the time, writing a post-it and putting it on your desk, helping you make class decisions)
- Ask your students to teach you something they do better than you do
- Delegate responsibilities to students that involve trust and tell them why you are giving that job to them specifically (ex. *"I love that I can trust you to grab my phone from my bag, can you bring it to me real quick? Thanks Love"*)
- Boast to parents about how helpful a student was when they show you or a classmate care
- Link caregiving to later life (ex. *"Wow you are going to be one great husband one day!"*)
- Validate how responsible your students are to other people aloud and in front of them

Tip 3. Ask Questions

One of the most common relationship traps is when students feel they have no say, no control or are not being heard. One of the easiest ways to prevent this feeling is by getting into the habit of asking questions instead of giving directives, accusations or assumptions. Some examples include:

- *"Is there something you want to talk to me about?"*
- *"Are you ok?"*
- *"Is there something you need that I can help you with?"*
- *"What did you want to happen?"*

- *"When did you start to feel upset?"*
- *"Where is the best place to go for that?"*
- *"How would you like to go about doing this?"*
- *"Is there a better way for me to help you here?"*
- *"What would work best for you?"*
- *"Why didn't that work? How could we fix it?"*

Tip 4. Vet Yourself

Students are being taught, questioned, and tested all day in both implicit and explicit ways. Another way to build trust with your students is to show them that you are also actively engaged in your own learning. Involving students in vetting your teaching tactics, your delivery of instruction, and your social interactions with them is probably the most transparent way to prove that you value them as people, instead of merely teaching them as students.

You can involve students in vetting your teaching by asking them for feedback after lessons such as, *"How was that lesson? Was it interesting? What could I have done better?"* You can also allow students to give you feedback on your behavior management such as, *"Did you feel respected when I spoke with you before? Was it ok that I asked you that in front of the class? Could I have handled that differently and if so, how would you like me to in the future?"*

Tip 5. Own Up

Along the same lines as the above strategy, "owning up" about mistakes is another very simple yet effective way to build trust. If your mistake is something small such as giving the wrong answer or saying the wrong name, make sure to pause and identify this with your students. Saying something like, *"My mistake, I apologize"* is an easy way to both model pro-social behavior as well as offer a sense of modesty.

If your mistake is larger, for example, losing your own temper or disrespecting a student (if you would redirect a student for doing what you are doing, you may want to second guess doing it), make sure to provide a more serious ownership of this behavior. Honor students by taking the time to treat your own mistakes with the same level of seriousness and consequence as theirs. Take the time to stop, identify your misstep and apologize personally. Ask those students if they accept your apology and if they do not, allow them to explain why and listen to their reasoning. These conversations, when approached with genuine intent, can turn some of the most closed off students into children who feel valued, appreciated and believe you when you say you're sorry in the future.

Tip 6. Invest

How do you know someone really cares about you? Think about this question for a moment before reading on. Think about a friend, significant other, coworker, or spouse. What do the people you truly trust do differently than all of your other casual acquaintances? The difference is that people who care about you invest in you. They invest their time, their emotions, and their energy. As a teacher you might be thinking, *"I'm pretty sure I'm already doing that and then some for my students,"* but the investment that really matters is the kind that feels individual.

When a friend takes time to call you on your birthday instead of posting it on Facebook, you feel important. When your spouse shows up with flowers or your family makes a special sign for you when you come back from traveling, you feel special. When your boss or supervisor takes the time to write you a note pointing out a specific positive interaction you had with a parent, you feel validated. All of these small but meaningful investments of time, emotion, and energy translate into genuine feelings of value. You can do the same for your students by:

- Making positive calls home
- Writing small positive notes every now and then and hiding them in their desk
- Giving them a special nickname that affirms a positive, individual identity for them
- Creating a special signal that only you and they know to help them focus

- Showing patience when they are having a rough day and stating, *"I know your having a hard time but you are too important to me and I'm going to make sure we work it out."*
- Thanking them for small things they always do (pushing in chairs, saying thank you, holding the door)
- Stating their best attributes even on their worst days (ex. *"I know today wasn't the best, but with your brain and your dance skills, I know we can pop and lock-it-up tomorrow."*)
- Make them feel needed—remind them why your class wouldn't be the same without them and make sure it's positive.
- **On their worst day, invest in *them*, not their behavior**

Tip 7. Learn What They Love

It wouldn't make sense to teach without planning or present a lesson without knowing the content, right? The same holds true when it comes to learning not only what you're teaching, but also *who* you're teaching. Have you ever been to the doctor and they begin speaking at you instead of to you, using long, complicated terminology and making you feel like the wallpaper instead of the patient? On the other hand, have you ever had a doctor stop their explanation and make a real-life connection to something you know like a sport or a piece of kitchen equipment? They begin speaking to you, break it down into laymen's terms and connect to your understanding of something else in order to help you comprehend the new information they are presenting.

Sometimes students feel the same way in school, especially younger students. By doing just a little bit of research, you can gather incredibly valuable information that will not only help you connect with your students, but also engage their intrinsic interest more than you could ever imagine. The other good news is that this research is the least boring type. Find out what they like to watch and watch an episode. Cartoons, TV shows, movie characters, even popular commercials can all become powerful points of connection. Find out what games they like to play, what toys they play with, the latest dance craze, or the coolest new song they are singing and ask them questions about it. Make the things they love important to you and they will feel connected to you.

Tip 8. Listen . . . and Hear

Despite what sometimes feels like the endless times that you, the teacher, ask students to listen, they are equally as conscious of your ability to listen to them. It's not only listening to students, however, but also *hearing* what they are saying that matters for building trust. Students are the best detectives when it comes to bluffing and when you are nodding your head but thinking about something else, they know.

Especially in moments of redirection or behavioral frustration, it is immensely important to show students that you are not only listening to them, but also hearing what they have to say. Below are some concrete ways to do this during those times. A helpful way to remember these might be to post the prompts somewhere in your classroom (e.g., a sticky note on your computer, a sheet on the classroom wall, etc.):

- *"First of all, I'm very sorry you felt [insert how they said they felt] when that happened."*
- *"I heard you say that you [echo what they said], is that right?"*
- *"So you're saying that [echo their words] . . . "*
- *"I'm not hearing what you're saying, let's go over here where we can have a better place to talk so I can make sure I can really hear you"*
- *"Did I hear you correctly when you said [echo their words]?"*
- *"I'm listening, please help me understand what happened?"*

Tip 9. Validation by Saturation

Students are like sponges—they take in almost everything that they hear and see around them. That means that you, as the teacher, present a steady current of information for them to process and, unfortunately, their ears do not come equipped with "out of context" filters. Therefore, it is imperative that you saturate their auditory space with positive, affirming statements of validation whenever possible. This is not as difficult or time-consuming as it may seem. Simply stuff the nooks and crannies of your extra comments to students with compliments. Imagine you literally put on a pair of rose-colored glasses and anything you saw you had to compliment. Play a semisarcastic game with yourself if this feels terribly unnatural and make it a challenge. For example:

- *"I love the way you tied your shoes all by yourself, so independent."*
- *"That was a cool way to get up. Great job not knocking over the chair!"*
- *"How you managed to not spill that juice, even though you tripped, was kind of amazing."*
- *"Sorry, I was just starring at what a great teammate you were being, continue…."*
- *"Did you know that you are brilliant? Has anyone reminded you of that lately?"*
- *"Is that how serious block-builders put blocks away? I never thought of it that way!"*
- *"You are sitting up so tall. I think you might have just grown another inch!"*

Tip 10. Lawyer Up

Sometimes students feel like everyone is out to get them. Have you ever sensed this before? Students have often reported that they feel that teachers are just waiting to "catch them" and sometimes they feel like teachers are the "cops" and they are the "robbers." Whether this feeling is founded or not, the reality is that students sometimes need a reminder that you are on their side, even if they mess up. This is not to be confused with siding-WITH-them. Being on a students' side is like being their lawyer, in theory.

Even when defending a client who has committed a wrongdoing, lawyers have a responsibility to fight for their clients' rights, discredit any unwarranted accusations, and ultimately defend their clients from unnecessary harm. That being said, imagine you are a lawyer for your students. Even when presented with mistakes, wrongdoings, or even purposefully negative misbehaviors, ask yourself what you would do to defend them in front of a jury of their peers, parents, and the public at large.

What would you want others to realize or understand about this child, even when realizing that they have done something wrong? In the grand scheme of things, how could you defend their right to feel valued and important, even amidst making mistakes (as many small children do between the ages of 5 and 8 years old)?

Also, remember that, just like a lawyer, your *delivery* means everything. If your students don't feel you are genuine, they (like the jury) may not believe you. Below is a list of some quick lawyer lines you can use to defend your clients and in turn, allow them to feel so valued that they learn to defend themselves.

- *"You're so important to me that I'm going to make sure you get this done."*
- *"I know that it was a mistake, so make sure [your friend/your teacher/etc.] realize you're sorry because you are one of the good guys, not the bad guys, right?"*
- *"It makes me so mad to think that people might see you doing that and just make up their mind about you. You are so much better than that!"*
- *"No matter what you do, I'm on your side. I want you to succeed. Are you on your side?"*
- *"I see you. You are brilliant. Show everyone else what you can do."*

Tip 11. Learn your ABCs

At some point in your teaching career, someone will tell you, "You'll eventually run out of nice things to say to kids." You'll deny this, of course. However, don't be surprised if one day you find yourself constantly reusing the word "beautiful" to compliment your students. You may become astutely aware that complimentary vocabulary is limited.

When confronted with this very problem, the author went home, looked up a word for each letter of the alphabet that she could use to describe students in a positive way, typed it up, printed it out, and taped it to her desk. This list provided a refreshingly new way to compliment students.

This list, which now consists of over 100 words, is included in Appendix A as **P.O.P Resource 1 – Learn Your ABCs Glossary**. The best part is, some of these words are really high-level and will most likely spark interest from your kids, which will cause them to question what the word means. When they ask for the definition of a certain word, you will then get to tell them (thus further extending their compliment time), and they will learn a new vocabulary word while feeling incredibly proud to have earned a compliment!

VERBAL STRATEGIES

Strategy 2: Correct and Connect

When most teachers engage in verbal redirection, without even realizing it, they actually engage in verbal reescalation. In other words, the standard response to a student calling out, hitting another student, or grabbing at something they aren't supposed to is usually, "Stop doing that!" or "Stop [insert undesirable action the student is doing]."

Unfortunately, with this response, the last thing the student hears is either an extremely vague term (e.g., "*that*") or a repeating of the undesirable behavior itself (e.g., "stop *hitting*"). While this may seem logical to an adult, to a child who is still learning how to process language cues, their memory processes the last thing they heard, or the undesirable behavior. What we really want is for students to process the replacement behavior and do that instead.

The "correct and connect" verbal strategy is like a math equation for pro-social replacement behaviors where order matters. By providing students with productive content first, followed by supportive praise last, what they hear is first productive then positive. You name the replacement behavior that you would like the student to perform first (i.e. *Correct*) and then provide a supportive comment that motivates their intrinsic sense of belonging second (i.e. *Connect)*. You are *correcting* the negative behavior objectively, and then *connecting* positive feedback to the student subjectively.

For example, if the student is tapping their pencil repeatedly on the table instead of using it to do their work, you would first correct the behavior objectively and provide the pro-social replacement behavior by saying, "*Ty, could you please use your pencil to write with instead of tapping it . . . *" Then, to insert the sense of belonging we just discussed (who doesn't like a cherry on their sundae?) finish this redirection by connecting positively to the student. For example, "Ty, could you please use your pencil to write with instead of tapping it . . . *so that I can see what amazing ideas you have in that imagination of yours!*"

While this second part may seem unnecessary, your student will be far more likely to respond positively when they feel more positive about themselves. As you may already know, when a student feels embarrassed or accused, they are more likely to seek revenge than reinforcement. Many students are completely capable of following a "stop" redirection, but will refuse to because of the negative perception they feel from their teacher. Their use of self-control hinges directly on their sense of belonging, therefore, when they don't feel as though they belong, they will *not* follow your most basic directions.

Beware of the "But-Rule"

Another word to the wise—be careful to consider the age-old "but-rule." The "but-rule" goes as follows: you give a student a compliment and then you say "but" at the end. For instance, "Ty, I know you are trying to do the right thing, **but** *you need to stop tapping that pencil over and over again*." While you intended to say something positive to that student, the last thing that he heard was negative, which will unfortunately be the thing he remembers.

Think of this interaction the same as if you were trying to nuke a baked potato by wrapping it in aluminum foil and popping it in the microwave. One of two things would happen—either the foil would begin to spark and start a fire or the microwave would short-circuit and shut down. Sometimes, the same result can occur when we use "but . . . " after giving a student positive praise. It will either short-circuit your exchange, making them feel anxious, or simply confuse them, causing them to shut down.

Alternatively, when you objectively correct the students' behavior first, and then subjectively connect with the student last, you are ripping that annoying negative label off of the student and replacing it with one that feels good, almost inviting the child to want to impress instead of merely comply with your direction. Better still, not only detaching guilt from redirection, you are now also including confidence by adding a positive word as the last word the child hears as well as the rest of the class.

Beware of the "Sinister Whisper"

Another tactic teachers sometimes use thinking that they are being positive, when really this is just another short-circuit in disguise, is the "Sinister Whisper" tactic. Many teachers utilize a simple whisper voice with children (instead of yelling) to do just the opposite of connecting and think that they have really done that student a service.

For example, a teacher choosing to whisper to a student, "I need you to get out of my classroom right now . . . " obviously did not prevent that student from feeling devalued. Simply lowering your voice and changing your prosody does not substitute for the actual words that you choose to use. This is just another thing to keep in mind when the biology of stress works against us.

The fact is, whatever you are saying is the important thing. Simply saying, something in a quieter tone does not change *what* that student is hearing, but when you change what you're saying and choose to connect with the student, even in times of correction, that can truly change the way a student feels and responds for the better. A simple way to determine if your choice of words feels genuine is to simply ask your audience. Once you're done speaking with a student, ask them if they felt respected or not. If they say no, ask them for feedback on how you can change that. You would be surprised how many times students react positively just from having been asked this question!

Back to the Big Picture

The *Correct and Connect* strategy can be very powerful when working with students who struggle with self-esteem and could really benefit from an extra pick-me-up (perhaps a student who is constantly being bombarded with negative redirections or labeled as the "bad apple"). For these students, taking any chance you can to positively validate their sense of belonging is huge!

Sometimes a student may act out as a call for attention. Perhaps this child is one of seven siblings and he or she is always vying for the attention of his or her parents at home, but rarely receives it. As the teacher, your verbal interaction with him might be one of the only one-to-one adult–child interactions he receives all day. Understanding this, if you have a chance, even when that child is doing something wrong, to make it a positive exchange, wouldn't you want to take that opportunity?

Let's finish this strategy with some interactive visualization. Please imagine the following scenario. You are assembling IKEA furniture, a simple, 3-drawer dresser. You have been at this endeavor for a lengthy amount of time and you still cannot seem to translate the condescendingly simple pictorial directions. In your frustration, you do not realize that you are still holding a hammer and as you throw your hands up in despair, you gouge a giant hole in the cardboard back of the dresser that you had been working so hard to assemble. Isn't that frustrating?

A couple of questions: What was the purpose of the hammer? To *assemble* the dresser, right? What ended up happening as a result of your frustration? The hammer ended up *destroying* the very dresser you were hoping to assemble.

Compare this situation to that of your students. If we use verbal directions as our tool or "hammer" to build student learning, we want to be sure to use that tool carefully and productively so we can assemble positive outcomes. However, when we are stressed out, sometimes our negative emotions can act with unforeseen force behind our verbal directions. The result is much like that of gouging a giant hole with a hammer instead of using it to carefully assemble.

Key Points

The learning that we want to build for students is often dismantled when we insert negative emotion into verbal redirection.

For more examples of problem behaviors, social skills connections, and correct and connect redirections, see Appendix A, **P.O.P Resource 2 – Correct and Connect Redirection Glossary.**

Strategy 3: Executive Questioning

Another verbal strategy is the use of "Executive Questioning." This clever strategy acts almost as a form of verbal ju-jitsu for student problem solving. The name "Executive Questioning" stems from the executive functioning system of the brain. This system acts as the "command and control" center responsible for enacting self-regulatory and problem-solving skills also known as "executive functioning skills." By using simple questions instead of directives students learn to take ownership of their own problem-solving capabilities.

You can answer this question easily: In school, kids typically want *who* to do the work, answer the questions, and solve frustrating interpersonal feuds? Most would agree that kids usually want us, the teachers, to do the work. As teachers we are often more than willing to "help" our students by offering directions, answering questions, and solving problems *for* them.

Our common tendency to "over-help" can cause us to take on a judge role and hand out sentencing instead of teaching students how to be problem-solvers themselves. We also sometimes fuel the problem further by using the word "why" to begin our response to the situation. Think about it—when a student misbehaves, how many times have you heard yourself or someone else start their response to that child with the word "why?" For example, when a student calls another student a nasty name, a common response is *"Why would you say something like that?"* When a student is playing with a pencil instead of writing with it, *"Why are you playing with that pencil? You should be writing with it!"*

The most important thing to understand about the word "why" is that it inadvertently leads that student down a one-way street where resistance, blaming, excuses, defensiveness, or reaction are their only answers for you. That's not where you want them to go.

Knowing this, we can actively usher students away from the avenues of resentment, blame, and shame by using different prompting language instead of the word "why." The following words prompt students' problem-solving and self-efficacy skills:

- what
- how
- who
- where

These words are "executive" in nature because they cue the brain to initiate thinking about solutions and lead to steps forward instead of steps backward.

The following practice activity will allow you to get a better sense of this questioning strategy. Try asking a friend to help you practice this technique. Ask your friends to tell you a problem they are experiencing. For example, they could say *"I don't know how to change a tire"* or *"I lost my cell phone and have no idea where I put it."* From there, set a timer for two minutes. In those next two minutes, your *only* means of communication with your partner is through questions that start with "what," "how," "who," or "where." You may not give any advice, directions, or comments. You may only ask questions beginning with those four words to prompt them to problem solve. See how you do?

What you may have found is that it's a lot harder than it seems! This exercise helps to orient you back to becoming a problem solving *facilitator* instead of a problem *solver*. We don't give our students the answers to math problems in class and then expect them to take a test and solve those same problems independently. We need to build that same sense of independence when it comes to social problem solving. Using the strategy of executive questioning as a means to elicit student self-problem-solving rather than reaction and dependency is a great way to do that!

Key Points

When we use the strategy of "executive questioning" we replace ourselves as the "solver" (and often times "bad-guy/judge") role, and empower our students to become their own best resource.

For more executive questioning prompts, see Appendix A, **P.O.P Resource 3 – Executive Questioning Help Sheet.**

STRUCTURAL STRATEGIES

Consider the next two strategies as handy as a roll of paper towels in a Kindergarten classroom. When implemented, these strategies will allow you to be more positive and less reactive by providing you with ready-to-use solutions, even for the most unplanned problems (much like paper towels do). The most common side effect of negative student behavior is teacher frustration. This leads to a learning environment where survival becomes the primary function and creating a sense of belonging is seen as superficial.

Consider working for an employer who is only concerned about preventing problems rather than praising progress. If your daily routine revolves around worry rather than working, that environment can become toxic very quickly. The same is true for our classrooms. Understanding how to plan for proactive student processing will create a sense of classroom composure that you may have thought to be purely the fiction of pre-service teaching textbooks. Ready to be happily proven wrong?

Strategy 4: The Rebuilding Area

The "Rebuilding Area" is a concrete plan and place for this processing to occur. Whether students need to pause, shift, re-think, or recover, having this area set up allows teachers the ability to support a student who needs to process a misbehavior, while simultaneously continuing to teach the rest of the class. This is not to say that having this area should ever eliminate all one-to-one teacher-to-student processing, but this is yet another way to promote independent student problem solving while relieving yourself of the unneeded stress of stopping all instruction to "deal with" one student.

There are three main factors that determine the success of this strategy:

1. Separation of space
2. Presentation
3. Perception

1. Separation of Space

The first component when considering your "Rebuilding Area," or RBA as we will be referring to it, is giving your students a clear separation of space. This can take several forms depending on the age of your students and the space you have available. Using a comfy chair with a pillow and a sign that says "Rebuilding Area" facing away from the group or creating a partition by cutting out the bottom of a cardboard box and attaching the remaining open three walls to the top of a desk are just a few ways of doing this. Regardless of how you create this separation of space, the main focus is that this area represents a safe space to calm down without the student worrying about interacting with classmates or teachers.

How to Create Your Rebuilding Area

The first step for creating your RBA is to choose the space and the seating. You may want to use a beanbag, comfy chair, or desk with a trifold. Set the space up in an area of the room that allows students to utilize the space without interacting with classmates or teachers.

The second step is to create picture cards that either attach to a board with Velcro or can be placed into small pockets (especially for younger students). These cards will allow the student to independently process their behavior following a simple guide.

Separate the picture cards into three categories: feelings, negative choices, and positive choices. To be even more concrete for little ones, categorizing negative actions into "yellow" and "red" choices and positive actions into "green" choices often helps! In this system, "yellow choices" represent various low-to-mid-level misbehaviors such as calling out, not following a direction, or using unkind words. "Red choices" represent various higher-level misbehaviors where safety or serious emotional harm is at risk for example: hitting, climbing on furniture, kicking, or purposefully bullying another student. "Green choices" represent the desired pro-social behaviors that we want to see instead for example: using kind words, raising your hand, talking it out or using walking feet.

As the teacher, these categories are at your discretion, however, using color can help to differentiate between basic levels of positive and negative, as well as that gray (now "yellow") area in between, and can be extremely helpful for young students.

Another option is to make these pictures much smaller, and either mount or laminate them on a dry erase board so your students can circle them using dry erase markers and reuse the template multiple times. For slightly older students, you can laminate a template and have them use dry erase markers to fill in the prompts with their own words. You can also allow students to give their input and get their buy in. This enhances their perception of the RBA, and creates a solid sense of student ownership. Try asking them to draw pictures of feeling faces, allowing them to create the RBA cards by cutting out pre-printed cards, or help you to tape the feeling faces onto individual colored cards.

2. Presentation of the Rebuilding Area

The next important factor in the success of the RBA is how the teacher presents this area. This area is not a consequence chair, "bad student" seat, or punishment post of any kind. If you think back to your time as a student, when a teacher got mad at you and sent you for a "time out," what did you spend your time thinking about? You might have spent fifty percent of your time worrying about how you just looked in front of your classmates and the other fifty percent of the time panicking about what was about to happen next.

Perhaps instead of worrying, you were instead planning your revenge against the teacher that had just embarrassed you. Please take note: even an elementary math student can determine here that no percent of cognitive time has gone towards actually thinking about a pro-social solution to the behavior that caused the problem. Also, by the time you came back to the class, you were probably in far worse a condition psychologically than you were when you began the time out.

Therefore, it is essential to begin the year (or whenever you choose to implement this strategy) with a direct instruction lesson that introduces the concept of this new space and concretely teaches how to use it much the same as you would teach your students how to line up for gym class or hang up their book bags in their cubbies.

Introducing The Rebuilding Area

The RBA needs to promote a "helping" mentality. As the teacher, instead of being the enforcer and "catching kids being bad," you are encouraging a sense of student self-control and offering options for your students. You want students to feel good about using this area as a way to increase their independence, grow into better problem-solvers, and become the boss of their own behaviors. If you present the process from this angle, students will be more motivated and eager to use this area instead of being embarrassed and resistant.

In order to facilitate this process, try to recognize some of your students' behavioral triggers. When you see that a student is beginning to unravel, this is the opportune time to make a positive example out of a potentially negative situation. Using a prompt like, *"[Student's name], I see that you're starting to get frustrated and tapping your pencil pretty hard against the desk here. I think that this would be a great time for you to use our Rebuilding Area! You can calm down without getting in trouble, and also be your own boss and choose your own solution to help you get back on track! I think you can become a great example for our class and maybe even teach some other students how to control their frustration just like you did!"*

To see an example of the author introducing the Rebuilding Area, visit www.empowerprogram.net.

How The Rebuilding Area Works

If you were using picture cards for your RBA, students would use the area as follows. First, the student would choose a picture card that matches how they are feeling and place it on the template or processing board. Next, the student would find a picture of their negative choice or behavior and attach that to the board. Finally, the student would look for a picture showing a positive replacement behavior or "green" choice (if you are using color coding) and place it in the last space of the template.

For instance, a sample template or processing board might read, "I feel _____. I chose to _____. I can choose to _ ___ instead".

Using picture cards allows students to access this problem solving as an independent, step-by-step routine rather than a teacher-dependent conference. Also, this aids in students being able to verbalize the cause and effect relationship between their feelings and actions by using the pictures as a guide. This concrete tool also allows you, the teacher, to provide the opportunity to spend time processing without taking you away from your other students or from instruction. Think of this like having a social worker or counselor in a bottle (or board).

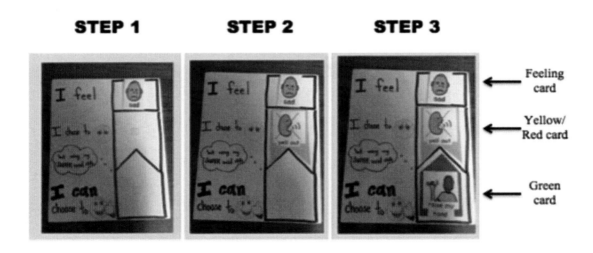

3. Perception of the Rebuilding Area

The final key factor, which directly hinges on your presentation of the RBA, is your students' perception of this space. If your students perceive the RBA as a space for thinking, calming down, and "rebuilding" potentially poor decisions into new and better ones, it can become a positive option for them. If they are complimented for using this space and prompted in a positive way, students will begin to use self-regulatory skills by using the RBA as a place to calm down and regain control without the teacher asking them to use it. You can now shift your attention to reinforcing their self-regulatory habit of wanting to calm down and regain control.

If students perceive the RBA as a punitive space, they will not only resist the urge to use it, but fear even admitting that they are *beginning to feel* the need to self-regulate. This self-awareness of trigger feelings is a huge part of building self-regulation skills. If students perceive that feeling to be the beginning of a consequence, they will harbor those feelings, ultimately leading to a larger behavioral reaction and negative outcome.

Finally, allow students to give input when you first introduce this area. When discussing positive and negative (or red, yellow, and green) choices, ask your students what they think and use those discussions to craft your RBA picture card content. Asking students to draw pictures of feeling faces can also be helpful in decorating the space as well as allowing students to create the actual RBA cards by cutting out pre-printed pictures or helping to glue or tape them onto individual colored cards can create a solid sense of student ownership.

For materials check lists and processing prompts, see Appendix A, **P.O.P Resource 4 – Rebuilding Area Making Suggestion Sheet**.

Strategy 5: Solution Sheets

This final structural strategy is the use of "Solution Sheets." These processing forms reflect the same purpose as the Rebuilding Area, and can be used in the RBA, but are now made portable and span a larger range of situations. Solution sheets can be used to teach prior to negative behaviors, to prevent recurring negative behaviors, or to process after a negative behavior has occurred. The primary benefit of these sheets is that they are a readily available resource for your students' use. They are meant to facilitate proactive processing and reduce the amount of time you, the teacher, need to stop teaching in order to engage in redirecting.

The second benefit of solution sheets is to give you a caring way to communicate with your students that both protects them from feeling "put on the spot" while also prompting the importance of paying attention to whatever problem they may be having. These sheets provide students with the ability to communicate their frustration to you in a real way, without having to verbalize their feelings aloud, interrupt your instruction or lash out for the same type of attention.

The final benefit of solution sheets is to provide teachers a way to give students privacy that feels genuine instead of utilitarian. When a student feels like they aren't being heard, that a teacher is not listening to their side of the story or that "no one understands them," students tend to shut down entirely. Instead, solution sheets invest students in feeling that they have a voice, a way to tell their end of the story and a longer time to talk to their teacher, even if that teacher is teaching at the very same time. The following will explain how each individual solution sheet works.

How Each Solution Sheet Works

There are four types of solution sheets: *VENT, RENT, REBUILD,* and *RESPOND.* The *VENT* and *RENT* solution sheets function as *preventative* measures, allowing students to self-monitor frustrations before they become problems. The *REBUILD* and *RESPOND* solution sheets act as *responsive* measures, helping students to process what happened after a problem has occurred and plan for a more productive course of action the next time.

1 – The VENT Solution Sheet

The VENT Solution Sheet allows students to "vent" or "get out" whatever it is that is bothering or distracting them from the lesson. How many times have you, as an adult, just needed vent to get something off your chest? We don't often allow our students this same outlet in schools. This leads to student frustration and eventually to negative outbursts. Providing students with a VENT Solution Sheet allows them to express rather than repress their feelings, as well as feel "heard" by the teacher reading the sheet. Though the student may not be talking directly to you, they will know that the things that they write, circle or draw on their VENT Solution Sheet are going to be read by you soon. This can make a huge difference to some children and can also reduce attention-seeking behaviors in the process.

There is also an area on the VENT Solution Sheet for students to draw what they felt was going on when the problem occurred. This serves two purposes. The first is to actively engage the child in processing the actions they chose during the problem. The second is to give you valuable information from the child's perspective on their perception of the situation from their point of view. This is often a big part of behavioral problems: the difference between what *actually* happened and what the child thinks or feels happened. By simply providing a space for students to give their perspective, free of correction, can mean the difference between "your blaming me" and "I didn't realize I did that?"

Finally, at the bottom of the VENT Solution Sheet is a collection of positive choices for the student to self-select before coming back to the lesson or sharing their VENT Solution Sheet with you. This promotes a sense of independence as well as concrete steps for the student to use in order to transition back from venting in a positive way. Remember also that this entire process, including all of the helpful reminders, is occurring while you are still instructing other students because it is laid out for the student on the VENT Solution Sheet!

See Appendix A for **P.O.P Resource – VENT Solution Sheet**.

2 – The RENT Solution Sheet

The RENT Solution Sheet helps students to appropriately ask for space if they are really angry or agitated. The name "rent" represents a need for the student to physically ask for space away from the lesson, from you, or from the person that they are having the most trouble getting along with *before* they actually engage in a negative response. This can be explained to students by discussing how adults can rent an apartment to live in for a year and then have the option to move to a different space. The idea is that when a student is too frustrated to sit inside of the classroom or at their desk to write a VENT Solution Sheet, that we are proactive as teachers and provide another option that temporarily allows them to have space to cool off.

Though this seems very similar to the concept of Rebuilding, the idea of "renting" space is to try and prompt this *before* a problem occurs instead of during or after. While we want students to use the RBA proactively too, "renting" doesn't require any processing, picture cards, or steps to communicate their thinking other than circling what space they would like to use to calm down. This can be less intimidating for some students and reinforce your position as helper instead of "giver of more work" when they just need a break.

This solution sheet is very simple in its design for that very reason. Students who would like to "rent" would ask (in whatever procedural way you have instructed them to, such as raising their hand or giving a signal) for a RENT Solution Sheet. Then, the student simply circles on that sheet which pre-determined location they would like to use to calm down. (You can write these into your sheets or use pictures.) The use of space separators, folders, or even sunglasses can also be used to give the feeling of privacy to students when you cannot have them out of your sight. In other situations, allowing a student to sit with another teacher or student can also be used as options.

When the student feels calmer, they will return to the lesson and can either write a *"VENT"* sheet explaining to you what the problem was, or simply begin positively participating again. Regardless of what specific options you choose to give your students, be sure to teach the specific procedure you want your students to follow before rolling this strategy out.

See Appendix A for **P.O.P Resource – RENT Solution Sheet**.

3 – The REBUILD Solution Sheet

The REBUILD Solution Sheet can be used shortly after an unacceptable behavior or action has occurred. The concept of the sheet is almost identical to that of the "Rebuilding Area," however, this time you have a formal record and documentation of the process. Just like when using the RBA, the student must go back and re-think the sequence and results of their actions. This is very different from the reasons for their actions!

Remember from the "Executive Questioning" strategy, we don't want to focus too much on the concept of *why* they did what they did because that causes students to be defensive, blame someone else, or resort to lying. Instead, the REBUILD Solution Sheet allows the student to back track and identify what happened before (antecedent), what happened that was problematic (behavior), and what happened as a result of that action of their choice (consequence). On the sheet, there is a clear, visual sequence of these three points in time. Students can draw or write what occurred at each moment in the frame, like a cartoon strip, giving both of you clear points of analysis for later discussion.

Showing students the distinctions between actions and reactions can be most valuable when using these sheets as the basis for discussion. Most of the time, it is not the students' initial *action* that is the problem, but rather their *reaction* to something or someone that else that triggers a conflict. Using the REBUILD Solution Sheet will not only help your students to recognize their triggers, but will also provide you with real-time behavioral data for parent–teacher conferences, disciplinary situations, and counseling scenarios.

See Appendix A for **P.O.P Resource – REBUILD Solution Sheet**.

4 – The RESPOND Solution Sheet

The RESPOND Solution Sheet addresses both recurring behavioral concerns as well as the issue of bullying situations. Since bullying has become such an unfortunate reality in schools, this solution sheet allows for teachers to give students a method of taking matters into their own hands without violence or additional problems. This solution sheet can also play a key role in documentation.

The name RESPOND is used as a direct opposite choice to "react." As students will learn from their REBUILD Solution Sheets, reacting can often lead to more problems, but responding represents a more proactive, productive path.

The RESPOND Solution Sheet helps students to choose whether they want to **confront**, **question**, or **report** the bullying instead of ignoring it. The nice thing about this strategy, as opposed to a teacher-directed student conflict resolution conference, is that the *students* are responsible for creating their own response plan. If the student who is being bullied feels unable to confront the bully, they can choose to report the bullying behavior and the teacher can follow up by assisting in a conference. The difference here is that the victim is still taking initiative to report the incident instead of waiting for an adult to take over. This can be a critical difference as they grow up and can be the foundation for them to move on to confronting or questioning the bully and gaining more confidence in doing so.

See Appendix A for **P.O.P Resource – RESPOND Solution Sheet**.

ABILITY

ABILITY CLASSROOM SCENARIOS

WHEN THIS HAPPENS . . .

Tyson and Julie – Version 1

After having a problem and receiving a consequence during recess, you ask Julie to take a seat at her desk and let you know when she feels she is ready to join the group again nicely. Julie is now sitting at her desk, angry, covering her face in her hands. You begin the next lesson by gathering the group at the rug while reminding Julie, *"You may join us when you are ready."* Julie just huffs and remains in her seat.

As you begin to take out several exciting materials for your demonstration, you see Julie looking up as she is enticed by your engaging manipulatives. She jumps up and runs over to the group. You stop her and say, *"Julie, are you ready to join the group now?"* She quickly says yes and pushes her way to the front of the group, grabbing at all of the materials. *"Julie, I need you to back up and sit in your spot so that we can begin. We are not touching the materials yet."*

Julie huffs and purses her lips, clearly frustrated. She stomps back to her spot and sits down, slamming into the student next to her. Tyson, who just accidently got hit by Julie's arm as she slammed herself down in her spot, says, *"Hey, Julie hit me!"* You look at Julie and say, *"Julie, that wasn't very nice. Apologize to Tyson please."*

Julie yells, *"I didn't do anything!"* and crosses her arms. You give her a stern look and ask again, *"I need you to say you're sorry though, even if it was an accident . . . "* Julie looks at Tyson and with a scowl and in a sarcastic voice says, *"Soooooorrrryyy . . . "* and then proceeds to say *baby* underneath her breath. Tyson mouth gapes open and he yells, *"Hey, she called me a baby!"*

You feel yourself becoming more aggravated and say, *"Julie, I don't think you are ready to come back to the group. Please go back to your desk and calm down."* Julie throws herself on the rug and screams, *"That's not fair! I didn't even do anything!"*

You feel exhausted and annoyed, as you just want to begin your lesson. If only you could wish Julie to her seat instead of engaging in this power struggle, which is now making all of your other students restless. You exhale deeply and decide to just move on while the other students continue to stare at Julie lying on the rug in protest.

WHAT IF THIS HAPPENED, INSTEAD?

Tyson and Julie – Version 2

After having a problem and receiving a consequence during recess, you ask Julie to take a seat at her desk and let you know when she feels she is ready to join the group again nicely. Julie is now sitting at her desk, angry, covering her face in her hands. You begin the next lesson by gathering the group at the rug while reminding Julie, *"You *may join us when you are ready. Just show me your positive T.F.B and we are good to go. Okay?"* Julie just huffs and remains in her seat.

As you begin to take out several exciting materials for your demonstration, you see Julie looking up as she is enticed by your engaging manipulatives. She jumps up and runs over to the group. You stop her and say, *"Julie, I'm glad you are ready, but I need that quick T.F.B check before you come back so I know you're ready!"* She purses her lips and goes back to her desk and puts her head down.

As you begin to explore the materials with the rest of the group, you see her again looking up, wanting to join. You continue with your demonstration and then just before asking the group the first question you say, *"Can anyone take a look at our friend Julie and tell me something really good about her T.F.B right now?"* Tyson raises his hand and says, *"She has her head up and is looking at the lesson?"* You air-five Tyson and say, *"Yes, she is showing really good facial expression – that's the F in T.F.B! Can anyone tell me something about her Body Position?"* You call on Janelle, *"She is sitting up and looking instead of having her head in her hands . . ."*

"Excellent, that's the B for Body Position! What is the only thing left for Julie to show us that she's ready to come join us so we can get this experiment going?" You call on another student who replies, *"The T . . . her Tone!"* As you air-five that student you say, *"Very good, Abe. We just need to see if she has a calm tone of voice. Let me check . . ."* You look over at Julie with a wink and say, *"Julie, are you ready to come back and join the group?"* (as you obviously whisper—*"remember to answer in a calm tone of voice"* and wink again). Julie says, *"Yes, I am ready."*

You have the class wiggle their fingers at Julie in silent support of her positive decision as you say, *"Now, let's see you show off that awesome, calm, body position as you sit in your spot next to Tyson!"* Julie smiles and sits down nicely, crossing her legs and folding her hands in her lap. You applaud overtly and say, *"Fabulous! Perfect 10! Who else can show great body position as we get back to this experiment? I need my scientists to have awesome social skills so I can call on them to help me with these materials!"*

ABILITY RESEARCH AND RELEVANCY

WHY DID THAT HAPPEN?

The Research

Notice in the previous scenarios, Julie's *initial* behavior and reaction didn't change. The difference was that in the first scenario, the teacher re-directed Julie to be "ready" without having indicated what "ready" looked like or sounded like. Different personalities, different backgrounds, not to mention mood, age, and temperament, affect each person's perception of what it means to be "ready" and it can be very different from someone else's. In the second scenario, the teacher referred to concrete social skills in her request for Julie to be "ready." She asked Julie to show calm "T.F.B," which is an abbreviation for Tone of voice, Facial expression, and Body position.

The difference is clear and objective. Julie goes from feeling judged by a teacher who is deciding whether or not she is "ready" to judging herself based on objective, visual indicators. These indicators, like a behavioral rubric, are the social–emotional learning skills that we will discuss in this chapter. When taught directly as content for students to master and use in the context of your everyday classroom vernacular, these skills become tools for positive climate and empower students to utilize them as powerful self-monitoring super powers!

The following section includes research that shows the hard-hitting evidence behind why teaching social–emotional learning is not just complimentary to your academic instruction, but critical.

Executive Functioning

Being aware of the research behind executive functioning is necessary to understand how self-regulation can become possible for students. Think of executive functioning as the "command and control center" of the brain. In daily life, we use five basic executive functions to command and control our actions. Those actions are:

- Self-awareness
- Inhibition (or self-restraint)
- Self-regulation of emotion
- Problem solving
- Self-motivation

Psychologist Russell Barkley, Ph.D., has conducted groundbreaking research on executive functioning as well as how this process relates to behavioral disabilities such as ADHD. He's broken down the common symptoms of this disability (inattention, hyperactivity, and impulsivity) as having clear roots in the executive functions of inhibition and self-awareness (or meta-cognition). What this research reveals are concrete paths to behavioral supports and strategies directly connected to these root causes.

The social–emotional learning skills that follow in this chapter have been created and categorized using this research as a foundation. To make the research kid-friendly, these groups of skills have been renamed as follows:

- Self-awareness skills become *SELF skills*
- Inhibition skills become *STOP skills*
- Self-regulation of emotion skills become *SIMMER skills*
- Problem-solving skills become *SOLVE skills*
- Self-motivation skills become *STRIVE skills*

These subsets both directly connect with the research and give students a way of categorizing skills for them-selves. The more skills they learn, the more they will be able to choose which ones to use and when. It's like giving your students a toolkit, but instead of just giving them a bunch of random tools in a rusty red box, you will be giving them a well-organized toolbox with compartments and illustrated directions for how to use each tool inside. They will eventually feel so familiar with the tools that they won't even need to bring the box because those tools will be safely organized right up inside their brain.

Emotion + Attention = Learning

How many times have you felt "emotionally unavailable?" For instance, you just broke up with a significant other and you have to go to work the next day. You show up, having only slept half the night, less-attentive to your nor-mal responsibilities, overall irritable, and constantly replaying visions of your past relationship in your head. You *might* not be as productive on that day.

We can all relate to having bad days, however, when you look at this emotional power over attention scenario through the lens of a child's ability to learn, the stakes become higher. Being emotionally unavailable for whatever reason can not only impact social behaviors, but academic ones as well. Students who are able to self-regulate their attention are able to pay more attention in class and also take on a deeper understanding of what they are learn-ing. Just like adults, when students are engaged and involved, they will retain what they are learning much more effectively than if they were distracted by negative emotions.

When we give students opportunities to be social within the context of academic learning, they have a greater ability to feel engaged by discussing, relating, and responding to their peers and thus utilize this ability to self-regulate for further learning. This creates a learning environment where negative emotions have less of a chance of interfering with instruction and social–emotional learning can coincide with academics seamlessly.

Why Reward/Punish Doesn't Work

Please take out a piece of paper and take this little quiz. Define the following words:

1. Undervisning _____
2. Pomaga _____ _
3. Siswa _____
4. Mokytis _____
5. Lucru _____

Come on . . . let's go . . . what are you waiting for? Just jot down the definitions. You are a smart person and you can clearly read this book, so why can't you define a couple of simple words? What's wrong with you!

Were you a little uncomfortable with this pop quiz, fellow "prepared professional"? Might you have come to the unfortunate conclusion that you may have never learned the definitions of these words *before* being quizzed on their meaning? Would having been *taught* the five languages that the above vocabulary words are written in helped you succeed? The nerve of you asking for such a thing!

Think about how you felt staring at that piece of paper basically gauging how "smart" you thought you were. Would you like to know what those words mean? The first one *(undervisning)* means "teaching" in Norwegian. The second *(pomaga)* means "helps" in Slovenian. The third *(siswa)* means "students" in Indonesian. The fourth *(mokytis)* means "learn" in Lithuanian and finally the last one *(lucru)* means "things" only in Romanian. So there you go. Your pop quiz actually reads: **"Teaching helps students learn things."** Interesting notion, don't you think?

The premise here is simple: it is much easier to succeed at a skill (such as the acquisition and understanding of new vocabulary words) if you have been taught that skill. The term "ability" is defined as, *"the capacity to do something successfully or an **acquired skill**."* For students, social skills are that capacity for positive behavior within the classroom.

The social skills in this section empower your students with the *ability* to become more account*able* for their own social and behavioral choices. How many times a day in educational spaces do you hear the word "accountable" thrown around? For instance, *"Well, he's just not being accountable for his behavior . . ."* or *"If they would be more accountable for their choices, they wouldn't get into trouble and I could teach . . ."* Reflecting on these common examples, the question becomes not "are they being . . ." but "do they know for what and how they are being held accountable?" This is a question of acquisition, *not* accusation.

As teachers, we think this concept is pretty obvious, but a lot of the time we assess behavior *without* providing content.

What's the assessment of behavior? If a test or quiz is an assessment of academics, what is the equivalent for behavioral skills? What about when a student receives a consequence for getting angry and yelling? What about when they get in trouble for not being able to compromise, and they throw a fit? What about when they rip up their homework because it's late and now it's not acceptable to be handed in? Is it fair to assess someone on something you may have never taught them?

Remember, the skill being assessed for behavior isn't the students' ability to do their homework or simply remember the classroom rules, it's their ability to *use* social–emotional learning skills to self-regulate their reactions to situations that are being tested. Consequently, providing our students with social–emotional learning skills that allow them the true ability to be accountable for their behavior is not only fair, but critical to their learning and your classroom environment.

The Relevancy

The big picture connection here links to the concept of Mastery, the second quadrant in the "Circle of Courage." When we offer students opportunities to show mastery in our classroom, they feel successful. Academic learning is riddled with these opportunities, however, social–emotional learning is seldom considered as an area for students to learn and master content in the same way. When students are given the content of social–emotional learning, taught the skills, and given feedback about their progress, social–emotional learning becomes a welcome opportunity for students to feel as if they have mastered something. This makes them feel more confident, inspires further learning, and drives self-esteem.

On the other hand, when opportunities for mastery are missing, students often avoid taking risks, become unmotivated, and give up easily. We can also see this concept of mastery become distorted when students become compulsive or succumb to the pressure of cheating in order to salvage a sense of mastery that they do not feel they can achieve.

The strategies that follow will allow you to provide many opportunities to students for mastery in the area of social–emotional learning. This shift from only learning academic skills to also being able to learn and master social skills not only improves your classroom climate, but also creates more avenues for your students to feel successful.

Relevancy in a Cultural Context

Data

- *"There are several benefits to students related to social and emotional learning. For instance, students are able to know and manage themselves better, guides students to ask questions and understand people who look different than themselves, and creates opportunities for students to find sameness among diverse peers"* (Durlak et al., 2011; Farrington et al., 2012; Sklad et al., 2012).

- *"In addition, adequate social and emotional skills allow students to possess more of a positive attitude toward themselves and others, reduce conduct problems and risk-taking behavior, and improve test scores, grades, and attendance. In turn, these skills provide students with long term outcomes such as, an increase in the likelihood of high school graduation, readiness for postsecondary education, positive family and work relationships, and a reduction in criminal behavior"* (Hawkins, Kosterman, Catalano, Hill, & Abbott, 2008; Jones, Greenberg, & Crowley, 2015).

- *"When students experience their school as safe, they are likely to perform well. Unfortunately, at many schools, students fear that they will be verbally or physically abused* (Astor, Benbenishty, Zeira, & Vinokur, 2002). *Students who witness such abuse may suffer academically, even if they are not victims themselves"* (Rivers, Poteat, Noret, & Ashhurst, 2009).

- *"Teachers who are prone to accepting stereotypes of adolescent African-American males as threatening or dangerous may overreact to relatively minor threats to authority, especially if their anxiety is paired with a misunderstanding of cultural norms of social interaction."* This leads us to ask, *"Why must advocates for students of color prove that African American students do not deserve unequal treatment?"* (Skiba, Michael, Nardo, Carrol, Reesce, 2002).

- *"Establishing and maintaining a positive school and classroom climate allows a school community to proactively prevent discipline issues by increasing the strength and the quality of classroom activities. Implicit in this approach is the assumption that participating in well-managed classroom activities encourages self-discipline by teaching students about what is possible through cooperation and coordination with others. It also provides the essential conditions for caring, support, clear expectations, and guidance that nurture healthy student development and motivation"* (Safe Support Learning, 2016).

Questions

In the first section, you reflected on the data presented by questioning your personal feelings and reactions. Now, let's shift towards a broader, societal perspective. To what degree do you feel that society (also your school system or the broader educational system you are working within) reflects a "socialized bias" in light of the above information? How do you see internalized racism, stereotypes of class and disability, or distrust of marginalized youth play a role in the learning-environments of your students? Given the clear positive effects of providing a proactive school climate where social–emotional learning is present and the clear negative effects of accepting stereotypes of marginalized youth in a reactive, disciplinary manner, how do you think social–emotional learning connects to larger issues of social justice? Do you feel that educational spaces should consider this when planning for their climate and behavioral supports? Can you, as a single person, positively affect the answer to this question?

The Good News . . .

The answer to the last question is simple—yes, you can. While school systems and other large spaces of education may feel largely bureaucratic and closed to internal change at times, any educator on any day can become a positive fulcrum for a child. Your knowledge of "socialized bias" and willingness to do something about it does not give you automatic power to change an entire systematized set of norms, but it will give you the power to shift that sense of imbalance for that child. By acknowledging the general lack of social–emotional learning instruction most students receive, even though the benefits are clearly positive, you now have the opportunity to tilt the proverbial seesaw in favor of prioritizing this need in your classroom.

You can actively make this a priority within your classroom, even within your school or other educational systems' set of required rules and procedures. You are single-handedly creating student capacity and empowering positive change. You are actively advocating for positive, quality learning outcomes for your students within a very small, albeit very powerful, space by thoughtfully challenging the lack of these supports and instead proactively providing them.

This not only changes student outcomes in your classroom, but also changes the way in which students of different cultural, racial, and disability groups perceive their right to that type of support, even after they leave your class. This becomes a huge asset for students who may have only known the minimal level of support, or more likely, none at all. You empower students to advocate for themselves by modeling advocacy. In this way, you build capacity instead of just providing temporary care and concern.

The strategies that follow were written for *all* students, in order to provide them with social–emotional learning and executive functioning skills in the areas of self-regulation, inhibition, problem solving, handling frustration and striving to reach goals. When you can present all students with the concrete tools they need to learn these important skills critical for success beyond elementary school, all students will still be affected by the socialized bias—only now from a place of support rather than stigma.

ABILITY CONCRETE STRATEGIES

WHAT CAN I DO?

The following strategies will allow you to take full advantage of the research you just read. These strategies provide easy-to-implement ways for you to teach your students the functional social–emotional skills that they need to better self-regulate.

Strategy 1: Common Language Prompts

Visualize yourself moving through the following activity. You are the student and your teacher needs you to change something about the way you are behaving. To aide in this visualization, imagine that successfully following your teachers' directions is now represented concretely as a giant board game that you can stand inside, like hopscotch.

Unlike hopscotch, however, this game is very simple and only has four, square spots from beginning to end in a straight line. You are currently standing inside the START spot on the game (board). Written within the next spot is the phrase, "***stop*** *doing the negative behavior*." Written across the next spot reads, "***start*** *doing the positive behavior*." The final spot on the game says FINISH. If you get to the FINISH spot, you have won the game! (Please visit website www.empowerprogram.net for a video demonstration).

Now imagine that colored playground balls are being used to symbolize the cognitive information you are going to be required to process as a student. Your job, as the student, is to figure out what you need to *stop* doing (the negative behavior) as well as what you need to *start* doing (the positive behavior) while simultaneously holding all of the teacher's directions in mind (colored playground balls you must catch and hold, while trying to move across the game board).

For the first try, an orange playground ball will be thrown to you, which signifies each verbal direction you receive from the teacher. You must catch and hold each ball to show that you have heard and can remember that direction. Ready?

> "Stop doing **that**!" (first orange ball thrown to you).
> "**This** isn't what you should be doing!" (second orange ball).
> "**That** is not okay!" (another ball thrown).
> "You're doing **that** again!" (another orange ball gets thrown to you).

First question: how did you do? You may have had a hard time catching all of those "directions" one after another and by the fourth one, you may have dropped a couple of "directions" (balls) just trying to keep up! Second question: could you successfully move across to the second spot? In order to do that, you would need to "***stop doing the negative behavior***" as the first step clearly says.

For your second try, instead of being thrown the orange playground balls, which represent "this" and "that" directives, the teacher will name the behavior he or she wants you to stop doing. That should help, right? We will use purple playground balls to represent the teacher actually naming the negative behavior for you. Ready?

> "Stop **speaking like that**!" (first purple ball thrown).
> "You're being **rude**!" (second purple ball thrown).
> "Excuse me, that **voice is not okay** in this classroom!" (another purple ball)
> "You're **being rude again**!" (yet another purple ball thrown at you).
> "Uhhhhh, stop **talking like that**!" (a final purple ball thrown).

How do you think you would do this time? As the student, could you tell me what you were supposed to stop doing? If you said you should stop speaking in some sort of rude way, you can now step into the second spot! Next question: can you tell me what you should *start* doing? Remember, the only information you have are the directions you have been given from your teacher.

Clearly, at this point, you may not only be confused but also frustrated being stuck in the middle of the game board, having successfully figured out what you needed to *stop* doing, but having no idea what you need to *start* doing to move forward! You can imagine in this scenario that your teacher might also be very frustrated because he or she assumed that when they told you to stop yelling, you would understand that they also wanted you to start using a lower tone of voice instead. In the end, you were too frustrated trying to balance all these directions while your teacher was becoming more aggravated by your seeming defiance. Does this whole experience sound a little familiar?

Analyze the Experience

As teacher, what we sometimes don't realize is that when redirecting a student, we are actually asking them to do *two* things instead of *one*. The first is to **stop** doing one thing in order to start doing something else. We want them to stop the negative behavior, in order **start** a positive replacement behavior that will be more productive. This second part is often missing.

The orange playground balls you were asked to metaphorically catch in the first round of play signified what we will refer to as the "Pick and Peck Express." This is where the teacher picks and pecks using words like "this" and "that" in order to redirect a student. Clearly these words are very broad and provide a lot for the student to avoid, but no real path to follow.

Also, did you notice how the teacher was asking you to hold a bunch of different directions in your mind all at one time? This is a visual reference to what's happening in a student's brain. When they are trying to process all of these directions at once, without a clear understanding of what you want them to start doing instead of just stop doing, it can become frustrating. This might even cause your students to drop all of their attempts at following your directions, give up, and shutdown.

Key Points

When you use social skills cueing instead of vague redirections, you give students a common language that is both positive and productive for everyone involved!

But What Should I Be Doing Instead?

What if we replaced all of the vague or problem-naming directions from the activity above with specific social skills language? Imagine picking up all of those orange and purple balls, putting them into one giant gym bag, and zipping it up so none of them could fall out! That is precisely what social skills language can do for your students.

It allows them to hear one specific direction with a social skill already embedded. Since that social skill has been taught, reinforced, and learned by the student, they can then use that skill as not only a redirection of what to *stop* doing, but also a productive forward moving direction with specific steps for what they should *start* doing instead!

For example, let us analyze how things might have been different if the teacher said this: "I need you to adjust your tone of voice to a calmer one, please." It's positive, specific, and prompts forward motion towards the desired replacement behavior. Now you, as a student, know exactly what you need to *stop* doing (using a rude tone of voice), you know what you need to *start* doing (lower or change your tone), and you know how (by using the concrete steps in the social skill you learned). (Please visit website www.empowerprogram.net for a video demonstration).

Other Benefits of Common Language Prompts for Students

When a common social skills language is developed and shared with everyone in the classroom, this is not only beneficial for use by teachers, but also by other students. When teachers spend all day redirecting students, the classroom environment starts to sound like, "I'm the teacher, I'm the boss, and this is **my** domain." Referring back to the Environment section, there's little space for the feeling of belonging to develop here, and not a lot of a room for students to develop mastery, either. When we allow students to help prompt each other to use social skills through a common language, not only can we provide an environment of belonging, but we can also empower them to feel a sense of mastery surrounding the content of social–emotional learning as well.

When you combine this new sense of mastery with the belonging that we have already created using the verbal and structural environment strategies, our students can feel more involved and invested in the classroom community than ever before. When students support each other with known skills, they feel important and helpful. They become a social asset rather than a behavioral liability. It is this identity that can change the overall climate of your classroom from one of students who must follow the rules, to those who feel powerful by knowing what to do and how to do it. That identity is also far more exciting than simply following directions.

Using common language prompts can not only build a students' sense of confidence, but also cultivate a foundation for strong academic readiness. Common language allows students to improve their processing speed and also increase the rate at which they can spend time practicing and developing positive routines rather than strengthening negative habits. Pretty good bang for your educational buck!

See Appendix B, **P.O.P Resource 1 – Common Language Prompts Sheet**.

Strategy 2: Teaching Social–Emotional Learning Skills

In order to have a common language and common knowledge of social skills, we must teach those skills directly. The following section provides both direct instruction social emotional learning lesson plans, as well as supplemental activities to promote social skills acquisition and increase student engagement during that instruction. Also, as mentioned in the research section, the twenty five social skills have been organized into the five categories of executive functioning.

In Appendix B there are 25 individual student skill cards with checkboxes for each step and pictures of a student demonstrating that step for easy reference. There are also full color PDF copies of these student skill cards that can be utilized as digital classroom posters in the supplemental online resources (resourcematerial@rowman.com). For more information on these resources, see the Appendix B, **P.O.P Resources**.

How are the Social Skills Organized?

Self Skills The first set of social–emotional learning skills stem from the executive functioning domain of *self-awareness*. These skills can then be referred to using the student-friendly language of SELF skills. The five skills in this set are:

- Tone of Voice
- Facial Expression
- Body Position
- Personal Space
- Communication

These SELF skills provide self-awareness and also self-monitoring and self-regulation. These skills are the foundation for academic learning. The first three skills specifically (Tone, Face, and Body or "T.F.B") can be used as a solid starting ground to gauge emotional or behavioral readiness for any context. When students can understand and identify these basic skills, they not only demonstrate more self-control, but feel more self-confident as well!
    See Appendix B, **Lesson Plans 1–5 and Student Skill Cards**.

Stop Skills   The second set of social–emotional learning skills stem from the executive functioning domain of *inhibition* or *self-control*. These skills can then be referred to using the student-friendly language of STOP skills. The five skills in this set are:

- Keeping Your Cool
- Time and Place
- Waiting
- Asking for Attention
- Listening Position

These STOP skills allow students to develop and practice one of the most critical aspects of self-regulation—the ability to stop or inhibit their reactions or impulsive responses to typical antecedents. When used as common language prompts, these skills can help deescalate a potentially volatile situation by empowering the student with the control they are searching for. Instead of making a smaller problem even bigger, students can now use a STOP skill and regain control of the situation.
    See Appendix B, **Lesson Plans 6–10 and Student Skill Cards**.

Simmer Skills   The third set of social–emotional learning skills come from the executive functioning domain of *self-regulation of emotion*. These skills can then be referred to using the student-friendly language of SIMMER skills. The five skills in this set are:

- Handling Frustration
- Communicating Frustration
- Moving On
- Accepting Consequences
- Respectfully Disagreeing

These skills help students slow down and navigate frustrating or potentially negative behavioral situations using proactive steps rather than reactive habits. With these new choices available, they become more independent and capable of receiving positive praise in situations that previously granted them negative reinforcement (being accepted rather than rejected from a group due to the way they approach, praise instead of criticism from teachers and parents for demonstrating patience and so on).
    See Appendix B, **Lesson Plans 11–15 and Student Skill Cards**.

Solve Skills   The fourth set of social–emotional learning skills stem from the executive functioning domain of *problem solving*. These skills can then be referred to using the student-friendly language of SOLVE skills. The five skills in this set are:

- Communicating Concerns
- Joining A Group
- Compromise
- Problem Solving
- Choosing Who Goes First

These skills are crucial for navigating interpersonal situations, which make the majority of a student's school day. Instead of merely calming down, however, these skills provide student's direct action steps towards managing positive verbal interactions that lead to problem solutions. Simply learning to "communicate concerns" as opposed to fighting can really change the outcome of a small problem between two students. These skills allow students' to navigate the choices others in their lives make, including parents, teachers and peers.

Another benefit of teaching SOLVE skills is that it establishes an atmosphere of student independence and self-solving rather than teacher-directed discipline and redirection. This makes a huge difference in student ownership of behavior, classroom climate and general student engagement in buying into the rules. Allowing students to govern their own independence, the teacher then doesn't have to become the villain.

You will also note that the other social skills students have been learning from the other subsets serve as a helpful foundation. For example, in order to *respectfully disagree* it is important to monitor your *tone of voice*.

See Appendix B, **Lesson Plans 16–20 and Student Skill Cards**.

Strive Skills   The final set of social–emotional learning skills stem from the executive functioning domain of *self-motivation* and *activation*. These skills can then be referred to using the student-friendly language of STRIVE skills. The five skills in this set are:

- Identifying Goals
- Breaking Down Big Goals
- Strategies to Reach Your Goals
- Strategies for Working in Groups
- Finding Focus

These skills really ignite students' sense of mastery as they can enjoy the satisfaction of "taking matters into their own hands" by setting and monitoring their progress towards *their own* goals. This is far different than achieving goals set by parents or teachers because having a student set his or her own personal goals serves to build not just a skill, but a functional good habit for their future.

See Appendix B, **Lesson Plans 20–25 and Student Skill Cards**.

How do I teach these skills directly?

Each of the 25 individual social–emotional learning skills discussed above have a complete direct instruction lesson plan located in Appendix B. There is a step-by-step plan to assist teachers who want a scripted plan, as well as a **Master Teacher Lesson Frame** for teachers who simply want to run with a basic outline.

See Appendix B, **P.O.P Resource 2 – Master Teacher Lesson Frame**.

Breaking Down each Lesson Plan into Parts

The Logistics Section   The beginning section of each lesson plan contains required elements: common core standards used, objectives, and grade level. This section also includes a "Big Picture Goal," which gives the executive functioning domain that directly connects to that skill. The final component of this section is a list of suggested materials.

The Hook Section   The "Hook" or anticipatory set section of each lesson is meant to grab students' interest and engage them in a sense of curiosity about the lesson. This section answers the student engagement question of WHY. For the right-brain kids in your class, failing to answer the question of "Why is this important to me?" can completely discourage a student from paying any attention to the rest of the lesson.

In the first part of this Hook, you will be asked to "create an experience" that often requires the teacher to act out a scene, do an experiment, or catch the students by surprise. The second part of this section is to "analyze the experience." This is where students get a chance to make their own, intuitive sense out of what just happened. This also lays the groundwork for deeper connections, both intrinsically and conceptually, to the content of the new learning that follows.

An important note: you will see reference made to a "talking piece" in this section of the lesson. A "talking piece" can be anything from a ball to a soft stuffed animal to a marker. The main purpose of this devise is to have a tangible, visual prop which aides in showing who the speaker is and only the person who is holding the "talking piece" should be speaking. This can be a helpful procedure to practice and introduce with your students for other discussion opportunities as well as social skills!

The Teach Section   The "Teach" or direct instruction section of each lesson answers the student engagement question of WHAT. For your left-brainer students, this is very important. This section will introduce a student-friendly definition of the social skill as well as walk you through each individual skill step.

The Practice Section   The "Practice" section of each lesson answers the student engagement question of HOW. Guided practice gives students a chance to practice the skill steps within the safe confines of teacher modeling.

The Perform Section   Finally the "Perform" or independent practice section of each lesson answers the student engagement question of WHAT IF. This section allows students to work with the skill steps either in small groups or independently, enabling them to create their own meaning and practice each one.

Strategy 3: Weekly Frameworks for Instruction

After using the direct instruction lesson plans to introduce the social skill, there are several different activities that can be utilized throughout the week in order to both directly reinforce the social skill steps as well as provide practice opportunities at varying levels of independence as the week progresses. For teachers, this type of framework can be helpful for weekly planning. For counselors, therapists, and after school program coaches, any of the activities in this table can be utilized either in conjunction with the lesson plan or independently once students have a beginning knowledge of the social skill and steps.

Below is a brief explanation of suggested activities for a week's worth of reinforcement on the same social skill. A connection to Blooms taxonomy is also included to address how the activities build upon one another in a learning progression.

- Monday (Day 1)—Direct Instruction (Knowledge Level)
- Tuesday (Day 2)—Review Game (Comprehension Level)

- Wednesday (Day 3)—Steps in Stride Role Play (Application Level)
- Thursday (Day 4)—Media Madness (Analysis Level)
- Friday (Day 5)—Portfolio Page Assessment (Synthesis and Evaluation Levels)

Review Game Activities

The day following direct instruction, students can benefit from a simple review game. This gives them the most basic level of comprehension practice without going into too much detail about what each step means, or deeper into contextual use of the steps. This is merely a way to have students build mastery around what the skill steps actually are, like they would by learning the names and sounds of each letter in the alphabet before beginning to learn to read words.

Using props such as a basketball hoop (a simple Nerf hoop you can hold up, a garbage can, or box works fine!) and ball really build engagement and excitement for students. For this simple review game option, have students raise their hands to give you the first skill step. Call on a student and pass them the ball. If they get the step correct, they can take a shot at the net. If they get the shot in, you can write a point on the board. These points could accumulate to a weekly class total, again building teamwork and community, as well as a fluid competition opportunity to look forward to each week.

Other review game options include making a memory game with index cards. Simply copy the skill steps multiple times on index cards or cut from photocopied pages and lay them face down having students play memory for matching steps. Also, playing charades for each skill step can be fun and engaging.

"Steps in Stride" Role-Play Activities

The next level of practice allows students to apply what they have learned in context. We'll call this "steps in stride" because these activities literally provide an opportunity for students to practice their steps in the stride of typical scenarios that they will face in and outside of school.

One way to set this activity up is using a giant spinner of some sort. You can fashion one by drawing a large circle on a piece of poster board and dividing that into sections (usually 6–8). Label each section with various times or places where the students would contextualize using the social skill such as: (places) Cafeteria, Classroom, Gym, Outside, Bus, Bathroom, Hallway or (times) Arrival Time, Reading Lesson, Transition, Lunch Time, Recess, Free Time, Dismissal Time, etc. Now, put a paperclip in the middle with a pencil holding one end in place and have students flick the paperclip so it spins and lands on a time or place. When this happens, have them act out a scenario of using the social skill steps in that time or place.

This activity becomes even more fun when you have students demonstrate the correct way to use the social skill and then allow them the chance to also act out the incorrect way. This is not only fun, but will also present you with a chance to objectively notice if later that day, they happen to reenact the "incorrect way" instead of using the skill steps. Since they have already been through the motions both correctly *and* incorrectly, they now have that experience to refer to as positive and empowering rather than "you should know better."

Other "steps in stride" options include drawing bubbles on your board and writing times and places in each. Then give students either the eraser (if chalkboard) or a foam ball or beanbag to throw at the board. Whichever bubble they hit, they act out a scenario from that context. You can also pick times and places out of a hat or using a large dice labeled with times/places and have students roll for a scenario context.

Media Madness Activities

The next level of practice allows students to analyze the skill steps now that they have worked with them for a few days. Incorporating media (TV shows, Internet videos, cartoons, etc.) into this analysis allows students to use something they are extremely invested and interested in as the basis for contextualizing the social skill!

This has two main benefits:

1. Students are already watching these shows and already interested in their characters. When you link your social skills content to that material, students actually begin to connect their social–emotional learning content during times when they are watching the shows for entertainment and are more likely to think of new connections themselves.
2. Showing small clips of popular cartoon or children's TV shows as a part of your lesson will undoubtedly engage your students and maintain their attention during your instruction!

Portfolio Page Assessment Activities

The final level of practice that students can engage in is the synthesis and evaluation of their understanding of the social skill. This is usually where an assessment of some kind comes into play, such as a quiz or test. In the case of teaching social–emotional learning, you can absolutely utilize assessment, but in a much more creative and engaging way than by simply giving an end of the week skill steps quiz.

Utilizing multiple-intelligence based learning strategies can really bolster engagement! Having students create their own "Portfolio Pages" is a great way to both assess student understanding as well as provide an opportunity for different learning styles to flourish.

Each portfolio page idea connects to one of Howard Gardners' eight multiple intelligences and offers students an assessment option linked to their preferred intelligence. The following options are just a few examples of what you can offer students, but the sky is the limit, so be creative.

Multiple Intelligence	Portfolio Page Idea
Linguistic	Write a poem or story
Visual–Spatial	Draw a comic strip, poster or picture
Bodily–Kinesthetic	Create a dance
Logical–Mathematical	Compare/Contrast the steps
Musical	Write a song or rap
Interpersonal	Create a commercial with a group
Intrapersonal	Write a journal entry about your experience
Naturalist	Write or draw about the skill using nature or animals

The idea here is to allow students the choice of what portfolio page idea they would like to use and allow them to synthesize their knowledge of the social skill through their preferred intelligence. Portfolio pages can be displayed for others to view or sent home as weekly celebrations of their social skills learning. They can also be collected and used as a summative form of assessment at the end of the year where students will have created a complete portfolio of creative products featuring all twenty-five social skills.

The most important part of this final practice activity is not that students regurgitate the skill steps. Instead, the purpose is for them to synthesize and evaluate the skill within their own frame of understanding. This builds both investment as well as deeper understanding of their own learning process for other academic subjects.

See Appendix B, **P.O.P Resource 3 – Weekly Instructional Activities Grid**.

SECTION 3

MOTIVATION

MOTIVATION CLASSROOM SCENARIOS

WHEN THIS HAPPENS . . .

Abe and Maria – Version 1

It's now halfway through the day and you have just finished teaching your math mini-lesson. Your students are moving into their independent practice work. You begin to walk over to your small group table and simultaneously overhear Abe talking to his friend and playing with the counting blocks he is supposed to be using to help him do the addition problems.

You walk over to Abe and say, *"Remember, you are supposed to be using those to do your math problem, my friend. You can play with the blocks later during free time."* Abe nods his head and you smile, feeling that you have successfully navigated past this small issue and can continue your planned instruction. As you sit down to call your first small group to the table, you realize that Abe has completely ignored your redirection and is now building a tall tower, knocking it over, building it again, and knocking it over again—all while receiving more and more attention from his neighboring peers.

One of those peers, Maria, is smiling at Abe as he continues to entertain himself with the counting blocks. You decide to try and redirect Maria instead, hoping that this will lessen the attention Abe is receiving and give you a fighting chance to continue instruction with your small group. *"Maria . . . "* you call across the room, *"Are you focusing on your work or looking at Abe? I don't think he is making a very good decision, and I know you can make a good decision by ignoring what he is doing and getting back to work."*

Hearing this, Maria appears embarrassed and glares at Abe for getting her into trouble. Abe then sticks his tongue out, causing Maria to yell out, *"Stop it, Abe! Ms. Kendall, Abe is sticking his tongue out at me!"* You tell your group to wait at the table as you now get up, leave your station and go over to Abe and Maria to intervene.

You look at Abe, who is clearly unfazed by your former redirection and has no intention of changing his course of action from playing to working. You decide that Abe is no longer able to use the blocks and begin taking them off of his desk in a frustrated huff, as you explain to Maria that she can move her seat if she would like. As you begin collecting the blocks from Abe's desk, he begins to resist, grabbing as many blocks as he can and shoving them into his desk.

"Abe . . . " you command, *"Give me the blocks, please. I already told you to use them for math and you didn't listen, so now you cannot use them at all. You are distracting other students and now I cannot teach my group because I am over here with you. If you continue to do this, I am going to have to call your mother and you will need to have a consequence."*

In response to this, Abe yells, *"I don't care!"* and shifts into a state of super freeze, burying his head in his hands and refusing to move from his desk (effectively blocking your access to the rest of his blocks). You look at Maria, who has been watching the entire interaction instead of doing her work. You ask her to please move her desk, and she does so quietly, yet she looks concerned and distracted. You go back to your small group, who has now been waiting for 10 minutes for you to work with them. You sigh.

WHAT IF THIS HAPPENED, INSTEAD?

Abe and Maria – Version 2

It's now halfway through the day and you have just finished teaching your math mini-lesson. Your students are moving into their independent practice work and you begin to walk over to your small group table and simultaneously overhear Abe talking to his friend and playing with the counting blocks he is supposed to be using to help him do the addition problems.

You look around the class and say, *"Wow, I see one, two, three . . . so many students already starting their work! I bet you could score another team point before I even get to my small group table by having everyone looking just like these leaders up here. I see Maria using her blocks to solve the first problem already."* You then proceed to snake through the rest of your students who are at their desks, taking the long way to your small group table as you give thumbs up and verbally note other students following this direction. As you pass by Abe you whisper, *"As the king of free time in the block area, I think you can be the one to lead this whole class. Do you need any help lining up your blocks to work on the first problem?"*

Abe nods his head no and you say, *"Ok, then get right to work, my friend!"* Feeling that you have successfully navigated past this small issue, you can continue your planned instruction. As you sit down to call your first small group up to the table, you realize that Abe has completely ignored your redirection and is now building a tall tower, knocking it over, building it again, and knocking it over again—all while receiving more and more attention from his neighboring peers.

One of those peers, Maria, is smiling at Abe as he continues to entertain himself with the counting blocks. As you sit with your small group you call Maria over to your table. As she walks over, you tell your small group to take out their blocks from their bags and begin making groups of two while you talk to Maria. When Maria arrives you ask her, *"Is Abe distracting you? Do you want to ask Abe to conference so you can get your work done and also help him use his social skills by modeling how you use yours?"* Maria looks nervous and shyly shakes her head no.

You then ask, *"Would you like to ask a Peer Coach to help?"* She nods yes and you silently motion to Allen to come to your table. You ask, *"Allen, since you have been such a social skills leader today and are already doing your work like a pro, would you mind helping Maria as a Peer Coach?"* Allen proudly says yes. You ask him if he would help Abe to conference with Maria about the fact that she is feeling distracted because he is playing with the blocks. You know that Abe and Allen get along well, which is why you chose him for this situation.

Allen and Maria walk over to Abe who is still playing with the blocks. Allen asks Abe, *"Hey, can you come over to the Communication Spot with us? Maria wants to talk to you."* Abe looks suspicious, but walks over with Allen anyway. As he does so, you say out loud, *"Oh me, oh my, I feel another team point coming on. I love how I see my leaders working independently to solve a problem. Good stuff, people!"* You continue working with your small group at the table while continue to listen to the Communication Spot.

Abe and Maria step into the colorful shoes taped to the floor on the Communication Spot and Allen stands in the coach's corner. He asks Maria to start by saying, "Maria, can you tell Abe your concern?" Maria shyly says, "Abe I didn't like it when you were playing with the blocks because I couldn't do my work." Abe starts to roll his eyes and Allen signals him to stop. Allen says to Abe, "Abe, what did you hear Maria say?" Abe responds in a somewhat silly tone, "I heard her say I was being distracting . . . " Allen says, "Ok, so what can we do for a solution?" Maria is still looking at the floor nervously. Allen prompts Abe by saying, "Come on, man . . . " and Abe says, "I will stop playing with the blocks." Allen says, "Great job!" and Maria says "Thank you." The three students return to their desks.

You quickly go up to the Team Points board and increase the number by 1 point. You stop the entire class, point to Allen for being an excellent peer coach, and to Maria and Abe for finding a solution without needing a teacher or consequence and give a cheesy wink as you head back to your small group table.

At the end of math time, you walk over to Abe and ask him for his tracker. He hands it to you nervously, wondering why you want it since he feels he did a good job. You put a happy face into his tracking chart and ask him, "Why do you think I'm putting this happy face here?" He says, ". . . because I did my work?" You say, ". . . *and?*" Abe giggles and continues, " . . . and because I used my social skills?" "*Boom!*" you exclaim as you add another smiley face to his chart and continue giving the class the transition directions.

MOTIVATION RESEARCH AND RELEVANCY

WHY DID THAT HAPPEN?

The Research

What allowed teaching to continue in the second scenario? Did you read this and feel that you couldn't have handled the complicated steps the teacher took to handle a simple off-task behavior? The reality is, you very well *could* have handled the situation as the teacher and even had a less negative outcome than described in the first scenario, however, the question remains: what does that habitual pattern of "teacher handling" provide in the long term for your students?

The research that follows provides some helpful information about how to allow students to "handle" their own motivation for learning, contribute to the support and success of their peers, and even take some of that pressure off you. The main point of departure from the traditional teacher-controlled environment is to shift from a stance of "managing" *your classroom* to teaching students how to manage themselves within the space of *their classroom*. Once this shift has been made, you are both empowering your students to do more for themselves, while freeing yourself up to do more for your students. I assure you, this is possible!

Discipline vs. Self-Discipline

When you think of the difference between discipline and self-discipline, what are the first thoughts that come to your mind? Think of a time when you were disciplined. How did you feel and who were the primary players involved in the situation? Now, consider a time you felt you had self-discipline. How did you feel and who else was involved? How did you know the difference between the two circumstances?

The term discipline indicates the use of *extrinsic* controls while the term self-discipline indicates a sense of *intrinsic* control. The reason for your self-analysis in the paragraph above, however, is because—for students—it's not so much about the difference between what these two terms mean, but about the difference in how they feel when being applied.

When a parent or a teacher disciplines a child, that child feels as if they are being controlled. This is absolutely necessary in some cases, but it isn't the ultimate goal. Think about our ultimate goal: to raise and support independent, self-reliant students who will one day grow up to be independent, self-reliant adults. Therefore, the more a child practices developing self-discipline, the more confident they will become and more eager to use this skill into their adulthood.

Children who learn how to do a new move on a video game, tie their shoes for the first time, or read a big word without help become eager to do it *all by themselves*. Have you ever tried to help children who have just learned how to tie their shoes? They fend you off with the pride of a Trojan warrior. Why is that? Don't they want to get it done faster? It's taking them forever just to make the first loop. What's that all about?

The reason they are so intent on doing it *all by themselves* is because they feel a sense of pride knowing they have learned something new and can do it independent of an adult. This sense of intrinsic control is extremely powerful and creates a positive identity for the child.

How Does This Relate to Classroom Behavior Management?

This concept of discipline vs. self-discipline is so important because traditionally classroom behavior management has emphasized teacher discipline rather than student self-discipline. German youth worker Otto Zirker once observed, "When surrounded by walls, young people make wall-climbing a sport." Have you ever seen this in your students? You are merely stating what they can and cannot do and they seem oddly resistant to any logical boundary you have drawn for them?

Instead of focusing so much on simply providing disciplining *for* our students, the key is to use discipline to set the foundation for promoting the acquisition of student self-discipline. Instead of adults striving for control while student's battle for autonomy, the critical change is to show students how they can work with teachers to develop self-discipline as means of gaining the control and autonomy they desire.

Adult control can also become self-perpetuating, meaning the more adults control, the more they will need to control in order to maintain that environment. This presents yet another reason why developing student self-discipline is so critical. If you think about it, this is a "buy one, get one free" in the *worst* sense of the term. The more you control, the more you have to control and the less students want to show control themselves.

You may be asking yourself, "Well, I hope she is going to tell me some ways that I can go about forging this path towards student self-discipline . . . " and your answer is a resounding yes! In the Concrete Strategies section that follows, we will discuss easy-to-implement tools that promote an autonomous mindset for your students while building their self-discipline skills.

Self-Determination – Creating Stakeholders

Sometimes the most convincing research to a teacher is a real-life example. Ask yourself the following questions about your students.

- When one of your students wants to play a game on the playground, have you ever seen them go to great lengths to convince other students to play *their* game?
- Have you ever had a student who really wanted to earn something and began rattling off various things they could do in order to get it?
- Have you ever witnessed a student try to emulate an older student, whether this be wearing clothing like they do, copying a new dance move, or using slang?

Why are these questions relevant to the concept of student self-determination? They are all real-life examples of younger students trying to set goals for themselves. In each example a student has decided something is important to them, found people who could help, and ultimately, began planning to achieve the goal they set.

When students feel they are stakeholders in the process of creating, managing, and accomplishing their own goals, they are far more likely to buy into the arduous process of working towards those goals. The clear catch here is interest. Most students aren't the biggest fans of standing in a straight line, practicing their handwriting or cleaning up their toys. Knowing this, how can we still provide opportunities for self-determination for these rather boring but necessary tasks?

The Concrete Strategies section that follows will provide methods for offering your students a seat at the goal-setting table for both their classroom behavior and their academic learning. This section also outlines systems that tie student self-determination directly to student levels of independence.

These systems are different than a rewards-based token economy where good behavior yields stickers or prizes. While those systems are entirely appropriate for some students, the key to building long-term motivation and self-determination with your students is to involve them in the feeling of establishing and achieving their own goals. This lasts longer than specific incentive-based systems and reaches farther towards student independence.

Access

The final key to understanding student motivation is access. In the context of your classroom, access means the ease with which students can interact with the content you are teaching. Let's focus on behavioral expectations. In the case of teaching and reinforcing the social–emotional learning skills you just read about in the Ability section, making sure your students can fully access that content is crucial. It is important to thoroughly understand multiple ways in which you can increase student access for learning, resulting in greater student motivation for learning.

One of the best resources out there to both define and provide concrete resources for issues of student access is The National Center on Universal Design for Learning. Their website (http://www.udlcenter.org/) provides hundreds of examples, videos, and helpful tips. They describe all classrooms as highly diverse and reiterate that a "one size fits all" mentality for teaching is no longer applicable for our students. They define "universal design for learning" (or UDL) as an approach that minimizes barriers and maximizes learning. Understanding that each learner in your classroom has his/her own individual strengths, needs, and interests can be a daunting reality. What UDL offers is an analysis of how our students' brains process information and more importantly, how we as teachers can accommodate those differences for students without feeling overwhelmed ourselves.

The Logistics of Access

The brain processes learning using three broad networks: one for recognition (the WHAT of learning), one for skills and strategies (the HOW of learning), and one for caring and prioritizing (the WHY of learning). If we plan to provide multiple methods to support these three networks, all of our students gain better access to what we are teaching. This also increases their motivation to learn because there are fewer barriers during the process. When something is easier to access, you are more likely to attempt to begin moving towards it.

The UDL Center has an excellent short video that illustrates this concept visually (http://www.udlcenter.org/aboutudl/whatisudl/conceptofudl). Think about a mall or large public building of any kind. When you look at that building, it is designed to accommodate access for a range of individuals with different needs. For example, there might be a staircase in front and a wheelchair ramp on the side. The reasons and beneficiaries of those two different means of access may seem simple—people with physical disabilities need the ramps while people without those disabilities can use the stairs. Let's look at the design more universally, though. What about perfectly physically-abled people who use bicycles, workers making deliveries using a dolly, or a mother with a stroller?

The building was universally designed so individuals with a range of needs could access it. This is a helpful lens for viewing access for our students. If we step back from only limiting these considerations for students with disabilities, we increase the range of students who can benefit and also become more motivated to learn because of this improved access! The strategies in the next section will help you to design positive classroom supports as well as your instruction with the same universal access as the building described above.

How Does This Relate to Classroom Behavior Management?

To address the question of how access interacts with classroom behavior, think about how frustrating it is to lock your car keys in your car. Why is that so frustrating? Locking your keys in your car signifies a pretty clear denial of *access* to your mode of transportation, even though you know where you want to go, what you have to do to get there, and how to physically drive your car. When you are locked out of your car, you can't access the one thing you need to do all of those things you know you can—the keys. Also, how do you usually react? Does anyone throw a mini adult temper tantrum? Be honest . . .

For students, anything that gets in their way of accessing "classroom car keys" can become a huge behavioral trigger. Students that feel embarrassed because they don't understand the content as well as their peers sometimes act out to deflect that fact. Students that understand the content, but have trouble organizing their thoughts sometimes feel just as likely to react instead of patiently await help. Students who have a ton of extra energy and cannot seem to harness that energy in the classroom experience denial of access simply by failing to be able to hold the keys still long enough to unlock their learning. Regardless of why, these points of access directly relate to classroom behaviors and can be prevented with some support.

The Concrete Strategies section that follows will outline a few different methods for increasing student motivation (hence engaging access of the WHY network). There is also a P.O.P Resource in Appendix C that outlines simple yet effective tips for increasing student access for the other two networks (WHAT and HOW). This handy guide also provides tips for accommodating students with extra energy. "Too much energy" seems to be the most common complaint of teachers and also the most common link to student referrals for misbehavior. When using some of these simple access supports, you may find that even your most antsy students can better access instruction.

Key Points

Discipline vs. Self-Discipline

Use *discipline* to set a foundation and model appropriate boundaries. Spend more time promoting students acquisition of *self-discipline* in order to provide life-long skills, interest, and investment.

Self-Determination

Students who feel they have a stake in setting their own goals usually care more about achieving those goals. Creating an environment of self-determination in your classroom motivates students to take ownership of their learning and make positive behavioral choices.

Access

This concept requires us to look at potential barriers students may face that limit their ability to interact with what we are teaching. By taking time to support students in the how (process), what (content), and why (engagement) aspects of learning, we reduce their anxiety, increase their availability for learning and prevent those potential access barriers from becoming negative behavioral triggers.

See Appendix C, **P.O.P Resource 1 – Quick Guide to Student Access Supports.**

The Relevancy

The big picture connection here links to the concept of *Independence* and *Generosity*, the last two quadrants of the "Circle of Courage." When we offer students opportunities to show independence and generosity in our classroom, they feel connected. Students who feel a sense of independence as stakeholders in their own learning environment often act with more self-discipline and greater care for that space than those who feel they are being controlled. Once students have demonstrated a sense of independence, they also tend to be more inclined to show generosity. This sense of generosity isn't from arbitrary goodness of heart, but rather the result of feeling mutually valued and respected by their teachers.

Unfortunately, when opportunities for independence are missing, students often become submissive, irresponsible, or act helpless. When students take independence into their own hands, they can become reckless, defiant, and engage in power struggles. When opportunities for generosity are missing, students often become selfish, anti-social, and/or co-dependent. In either case, when the implications of both independence and generosity are not taken seriously in the classroom, these side effects can occur and then be translated as student personality flaws. The strategies that we discuss will help disconnect this negative association and reconnect you with your students.

Robert Carter, a professor of social work from the University of Pennsylvania, once said, "Hurt people hurt people." This quote has never made more sense in the context of comparison when we think of classroom motivation and the concept of generosity. If students who feel hurt want to hurt others, then by comparison, what would students who feel valued want to do?

Personal experiences prove that "valued students value other students." When we consider promoting a sense of generosity in our classrooms by modeling ways in which we support our students, the effects are much greater than students simply showing manners or not fighting with one another. When we truly value students, they understand and personalize that feeling and begin to want to value others now that they feel valued themselves. Finally, please remember that this process of building value takes time, even more time than you think is possible, but it is a critical and necessary piece of the puzzle.

Relevancy in a Cultural Context

Data

- *"Black students are suspended and expelled at a rate three times greater than white students. On average, 5% of white students are suspended, compared to 16% of black students. American Indian and Native-Alaskan students are also disproportionately suspended and expelled, representing less than 1% of the student population but 2% of out-of-school suspensions and 3% of expulsions."* (US Department of Education Office of Civil Rights, March 2014)

- *"African-American students and those with particular educational disabilities were disproportionately likely to be removed from the classroom for disciplinary reasons. For example, in a 2011-12 nationwide study where schools were required to report their school discipline data, the great majority of African-American male students had at least one discretionary violation (83 percent), compared to 74 percent for Hispanic male students, and 59 percent for white male students. The same pattern was found, though at lower levels of involvement, for females—with 70 percent of African-American female pupils having at least one discretionary violation, compared to 58 percent of Hispanic female pupils and 37 percent of white female pupils"* (Charter Schools, Civil Rights and School Discipline: A Comprehensive Review By Daniel J. Losen, Michael A. Keith II, Cheri L. Hodson and Tia E. Martinez, March 2016).

- *"Interventions, school-wide and individual, that use proactive, preventative approaches, address the underlying cause or purpose of the behavior, and reinforce positive behaviors, have been associated with increases in academic engagement, academic achievement, and reductions in suspensions and school dropouts"* (American Psychological Association, 2008; Christle, Jolivette, & Nelson, 2005; Crone & Hawken, 2010; Liaupsin, Umbreit, Ferro, Urso, & Upreti, 2006; Luiselli, Putnam, Handler, & Feinberg, 2005; Putnam, Horner, & Algozzine, 2006; Skiba & Sprague, 2008; Theriot, Craun, & Dupper, 2010).

- *"Students who have been suspended are significantly more likely to drop out of school and become involved in the juvenile justice system than their peers. Students of color, especially boys, and students with disabilities are disproportionately punished. Suspensions are often subjectively applied in such cases. For example, a significant percent of suspensions and expulsions are for trivial or minor offenses (e.g., "being disrespectful" or violating school dress code). Schools that approach school discipline punitively affect the overall school climate, creating a more negative environment for all students, including those without discipline issues."*

Questions

When you look at the above information, are you surprised? If so, why? If not, why? Think carefully about your answer to this initial question because your personal reaction creates a context for either your action or inaction moving forward. If you were surprised by any of these statistics, perhaps you haven't seen them in practice. If you weren't surprised, perhaps you are currently working within their context. Either way, what do you feel your responsibility is, as an educator of any kind, to actively question the role you play within them?

The Good News . . .

The fact that you are reading and reflecting for a third time on how your role as one individual working within a larger, more complex system can affect students is a good start. Discipline in schools has long been an area of discussion when we analyze how students of differing racial, cultural, disability, and socio-economic status positions are treated in comparison to their white or more privileged peers. Regardless of where or who you teach, your conscious effort not to turn this page in fear of this reality can be an epic gain for those students. Your willingness to reflect on your own biases, thoughts, and feelings on becoming a part of change in this sector of the system is where you can begin to etch away at these disparities.

It can be daunting to try and take on this task considering all that society, social stigma, and even simply your school administration could be entrenched in. This, however, is the reason why reading on is so important. The power you possess, as a single educator, is incredible if you treat it with the same respect you would other, more socially accepted positions of power. Let's be realistic—you're not going to change the world in a day, but you *can* change a day in the world of one of your students. Knowing this, allow the following section to provide you with tools to dig further into the mechanics of student motivation so you can design positive systems within your classroom, even if your classroom exists within a larger system less eager to change.

MOTIVATION CONCRETE STRATEGIES

WHAT CAN I DO?

The strategies that follow provide students with opportunities to exercise independence. Typically, the idea of tracking behavior, setting up class systems for reinforcement, and encouraging student leadership have been considered the domain of teachers. You set up a system, implement that system, and hope students will buy in. Unfortunately, as you've just read, that doesn't always work out.

The strategies in this section offer ways to involve students in managing their behavior and engaging as positive members of their own classroom community. This is in stark opposition to demanding students simply follow *your* classroom rules. Once students feel they have a legitimate stake in their learning and control of their behavioral progress, this sense of control becomes more evident in their daily behavior as well as their confidence.

Strategy 1: Visual Tracking

Do you currently own a cell phone? If so, do you have applications on that phone or do you use it only to make phone calls? If you have applications, what applications are they? Are they colorful? Do they make noises? Why do you have them? What function do they provide you?

This very important question was posed to remind you that, as an adult, we live in a world where visual tracking has become incredibly prolific. From timers to calendars, social-media alerts of every kind, and even applications that track your spending, walking, and eating—we are constantly availing ourselves with the latest methods of tracking our progress and reminding ourselves of important information.

Second question: have you ever forgotten your cell phone at home and had to be without it for the day? How do you feel? Ranging from slightly annoyed to completely debilitated, why do you think not having the ability to access your cell phone feels so uncomfortable? The fact that you cannot make calls doesn't fit that feeling because inevitably there will be a phone within reach for you to use, but would you even remember whose number you needed to call or did you store that information within the device you don't currently have?

The purpose of providing students with methods of visual tracking throughout their day is the same as allowing yourself to use your cell phone during your day. Visual tracking allows students to gauge their behavioral status, monitor their progress, and remember things they might forget without that helpful "device," if you will. When we provide students with systems that allow them to access these moving parts in a visual way, they are more inclined to want to be involved in their own positive progress instead of being disconnected or overwhelmed (much the same way you might be having forgotten your phone at home).

By involving students in a continual process of being able to visually track their own behavior, the choices they make connect directly with the results they see. Have you ever had a student complain that they feel as if teachers randomly impose consequences "for no reason?" How about students who feel that behavioral consequences are "given" to them because the teacher doesn't like them? Methods for visual tracking take you, the teacher, out of the role of judge and jury and back into the role of coach and supporter by involving your students in their own self-monitoring.

Whole Group Applications – Team Points

The strategy of Team Points is a great place to start when it comes to motivating students to engage in positive behavior as a group. Think of Team Points like the scoreboard in a basketball game. Teams use the scoreboard to gauge what they need to do to win. If a team is behind on the scoreboard, they know they need to make some changes, keep pushing, and work together in order to move ahead. On the other hand, if a team is ahead, both the reactions of the fans as well as their winning position motivates them to continue to play hard in order to push the score up even farther towards the ultimate goal of winning the game.

In the classroom, Team Points can be used to give group praise for any moment, large or small, that showcases positive "team" behavioral success. Some examples of this could include:

- When the entire class transitions from one lesson to the next smoothly
- Excellent walking in line in the hallway without being prompted
- Generous gestures made by individual students but supported by the group
- Students receiving a positive report for using social skills while outside of your class

In terms of logistics, you can set up your Team Points using an actual scoreboard or a simple tally chart. Another good idea to invest students even more in this group accountability is to have *your students* design or create the way the Team Points will be displayed. They can create a scoreboard and decorate it or come up with an even more creative means to display their points (the sky is the limit!). The best part is, the more students are involved in deciding, creating, and manufacturing the physical area in which the Team Points are displayed, the more they will be invested in wanting to use them.

You may also be wondering what the result of achieving Team Points would be? In kid-friendly terms: "What's in it for me?" The answer to this question can be determined in several ways depending on your classroom. One option is to set a specific goal (e.g.10 points) to try and have the class achieve by a certain time (e.g., end or near the end of the day). The motivation to achieve that group goal is then linked to a reward that benefits the whole group and connects back to the concept of how it feels to earn more independence. Some examples of these group rewards could be:

- Earning extra free time together at the end of the day
- Having the opportunity to choose where to have that free time
- Offering students a chance to decide on something for the next day (such as reading time under their desks with flashlights or choosing the read aloud book)
- Offering students a say in their seating choices for the next day
- Giving progress towards a larger group reward such as a field trip or special celebration

IMPORTANT NOTE ABOUT SETTING STUDENTS UP FOR SUCCESS USING TEAM POINTS

When implementing this strategy, make sure that you are setting your students up for success instead of merely provoking competition or pressure to "act as a team" or in order to earn points. This can be quite challenging, especially if you are waiting for larger group expression of social skills when there are still several students in your classroom who are struggling with those skills.

When you initially introduce team points, try making them contingent on smaller examples of group progress, such as students showing each other patience or generosity. You don't have to teach these skills, but you can praise them as a way to slowly introduce this concept to the group. From there, determine what type of group balance of general praise and skill mastery you want to achieve and use your students' reactions to being given Team Points to determine if you need to push farther or pull back.

Individual Applications – Student Tracking Sheets

While it's wonderful when we can praise communal positive behavior, more times than not student behavior is much more about individual choices and accountability. This is where using the same visual tracking strategy can be applied to each student. Using the Student Tracking Sheets introduced next is a way to both track individual progress data for each student while using a template (the tracking sheet) that can be reproduced and used for everyone. The tracking sheets that follow allow you to choose what type of visual tracking would best fit your students or vary the types of sheets you use for different students in different situations.

SIMPLE STUDENT TRACKER

The *Simple Student Tracker* can be used for tracking basic daily social skills progress or for any other goal a student is working to achieve. This tracker consists of three basic areas:

1. An area for the student to write and draw their goal for the day
2. An area to cut and paste or copy their social skill card or write the steps
3. An area to track their positive choices towards that goal

The purpose of this "simple" tracker is to guide students towards positive behavioral choices while giving them a visual reminder of how to make those choices using the social skills they are learning. The tracking section is meant to show progress towards the goal of exhibiting or practicing the social skill. This way students look forward to using the tracker to "show what they know" instead of feeling like this is a way to catch them making mistakes or a "teacher tattle-tale-tool," so to speak.

Try and avoid using the tracking section to indicate negative behaviors. A lack of green checks or happy faces does just as much to show a lack of progress than the addition of a ton of red checks or unhappy faces. The former just plunges students further into feeling that positive progress in unattainable for them. The use of accounting for specific negative behaviors for documentation is included in the third tracker discussed later.

The other reason this is called the "simple" tracker is because you can use it for a number of different reasons. As indicated above, the tracker is pre-formatted to coincide with direct social skills instruction, as shown by the specific space to include the social skills steps or card. This space can also be used for anything else you would like to track in a positive way. It can be used for therapeutic goals, academic goals, home goals, and afters-chool program goals as well!

SCHEDULE STUDENT TRACKER

The *Schedule Student Tracker* is slightly more specific as it organizes the students' progress throughout the day using a schedule format. This tracker consists of four basic areas:

1. An area for the students to write and draw their goals for the day
2. An area to include a time schedule of daily activities as well as a color scale
3. A "Helping Space" on the back with an area for social skill steps and reminders
4. An area for analysis or "How did I do?" where students can measure their progress

This tracker lends itself to school situations where students rely on routine and timing to help them determine what is coming next and what they have already done. This also works well to support students with various disabilities involving sensitivity to time such as Autism or ADHD, or students who need their day broken down into smaller chunks.

This tracker can be filled in once and photocopied for the daily schedule of the class or with a customized schedule for a specific student. The clock pictures help students to evaluate their own sense of time (as well as help them learn how to tell time by matching the picture of the clock on the tracker with the clock in the classroom). There is also a space for digital time or time spans to be included.

The "Color Scale" that is referred to is the other key part of this tracker. It includes a space for the teacher to rate the students' behavior using the colors green, yellow, and red. These colors help students see their behavioral accountability throughout the day. This is also a great tool for data and documentation for behavioral progress that can be included in reports, used as a communication tool for parents, and most importantly, used to accumulate visual progress to show students themselves!

The "Helping Space" on the second page of this tracker gives students an opportunity to plan ahead. It includes a space for copying steps from a useful learned social skill that may help them that day (or for teachers to copy/paste a social skills card from Appendix B). It also includes spaces for them to write what they can do if they need help or become upset. This is a great tool for teachers who may find themselves feeling like a broken record (i.e. *"If you need help please raise your hand . . . "*) as they can simply prompt students to flip their tracker over and remind themselves what they wrote or drew. This is very empowering to students who can then realize they can remind themselves about how to get positive praise by navigating their day more independently using their handy tracker!

The final area on this tracker is labeled "How did I do?" This space allows students to count their total number of greens, yellows, and reds from the day and see how they did. You will notice that this tracker is not tied to a reward system or end total for each color. This is simply an area to check in on progress and open discussions if needed. As the teacher, you may use a certain number of colors to correlate to a class privilege or reward, but that is completely up to you!

GOAL–REWARD STUDENT TRACKER

The *Goal–Reward Student Tracker* is the most specific as it directly links a specific goal or visual behavior to a specific reward or positive outcome for the student. This tracker consists of four basic areas:

1. An area for students to break down their behavioral goals into three categories:
   GREEN—Goal behaviors to try and show throughout the day
   YELLOW—Behaviors to work on improving
   RED—Behaviors to knowingly try not to use
2. An area for visually setting a reward to earn
3. An area to track their use of each category of behavior throughout the day
4. An area to analyze their progress towards their goal and decide if they earned the reward

This tracker is very useful for students who are on a specific behavior plan or need more specific reinforcement that takes into account frequent negative behaviors as well as their goal of achieving positive behaviors. This tracker is not meant to harp on those negative behaviors. It is designed to help both the student and the teacher to include those negative behaviors as a measure of continuing progress, with the ultimate goal being improvement.

It is also helpful for the students themselves to feel that they are included in planning for and documenting their own behaviors, including those negative choices they are working to improve. This perspective can mean the difference between a tracker that students view as a "teacher-tattle-tool" and one that they have control over. While you, the teacher, may still be the one helping to guide them towards verbalizing their areas for improvement, having the student write or draw these areas of accountability themselves can vastly change their sense of self-determination and accountability. Seeing their handwriting or drawing instead of yours can be the key to passing along this accountability in a neutral, yet real way.

Finally, the area where the student draws himself or herself showing the positive goal behavior and earning their chosen reward can be equally as powerful for motivation. This picture drawing allows students of any age or ability to access their own planning. It also gears their brain to see what they want to achieve before the day begins. As the day progresses, this picture will provide the teacher a handy visual to remind students of what they want to achieve as well as how to achieve it!

About Rewards

The topic of "rewards" for behavior can be a source of major tension between teachers, parents, students, and especially, peers. It is important to establish that the rewards used to motivate positive student behavior always connect to the pro-social skills that need be used to receive those rewards. For example, while earning a pizza party or special lunch is very motivating for students, how is this connected to using pro-social skills effectively? It may not be. This reward may simply be a *token* for progress that is exciting and valuable to that student. While tokens can be effective, you also run the risk of beginning a cycle of "If you do ___, you get ___" with students and that cycle, in the long run, will prove ineffective.

In order to avoid that trap, try to pair goals and rewards together. Have students set a goal for themselves and plan to achieve that goal by showing positive behavioral progress or using social skills. Use trackers to then help them monitor their progress and, in the end, if they have achieved their goal (which should be stated in the language of pro-social skills not tangible token rewards) they can connect that success with having the opportunity to enjoy a reward.

To bring this back to the pizza party example, instead of saying to the student, "If you earn 10 green checks each day, you get a pizza party on Friday" instead try starting the conversation this way: "When you use the social skill of problem solving instead of fighting with your peers, you might actually enjoy playing with them during free time. If we set a goal for you to work on using that social skill, what do you think would be a great way to celebrate becoming better at working with your peers? Maybe you could celebrate by having a pizza party to enjoy time together at the end of this long week of school?"

Although this may seem like semantic strategy, the connection becomes contextual for students. They are not individuals trying to acquire token prizes for individual actions. Instead, by making the connection between goals and rewards contingent on the use of social skills, you now create an environment where students achieve together and celebrate that social–emotional success within a social–emotional space. This connection both avoids the "If I do ___, I get ___" epidemic, and fosters a genuine motivation for students to work together using the social skills they are learning.

Key Points

- *Simple Student Tracker*– To track use of social skill or specific behavior easily to provide measurable data
- *Schedule Student Tracker* – To track use of social skill or general behavior using color scale to provide measurable data. This tracker also organizes data by time of day, breaking the day into smaller chunks
- *Goal–Reward Student Tracker* – To track use of social skill as a specific goal behavior, while having students pre-plan to avoid negative behaviors and provide measurable data

---

Strategy 2: Independence Level Choices

As mentioned in the Research and Relevancy segment, students who feel a sense of self-determination are far more likely to act in ways that increase their ability to gain further independence. The strategy of providing Independence Level Choices gives students a concrete path towards gaining that independence. It also offers students a genuine chance to control their academic experience through choice. This strategy uses simple yet specific labeling language to help students classify the behavioral choices they make into one of two categories: independent or dependent.

What are Independence Level Choices?

The strategy of Independence Level Choices shows students the direct benefit of making positive, behavioral choices by using the language of "independent" and "dependent" to connect those behavioral choices with subsequent academic privileges. This categorizing language feels neutral (as opposed to labeling choices as either "bad" or "good") while being specific in function. By labeling a student's choice of behavior as "independent" you are verifying their independent use of learned social skills and decision to interact positively with peers. By labeling a student's choice of behavior as "dependent" you are instead reminding the student that they may still need to *depend* on a teacher or more structured option to help them apply the social skills they have learned in order to make more positive choices or navigate interpersonal situations.

This sense of *Dependence vs. Independence* presents very different options for students as compared to saying their choice was "good" or "bad." Words like good and bad place the teacher in control, while words like independent and dependent place the student in control. This distinction is huge when it comes to a students' perception of self-control. Students who perceive themselves to be in control of a situation tend to be more self-determined, show greater self-discipline and make more independent choices than those who perceive that others are controlling them.

A perfect example of this can be seen when comparing the self-directed behaviors of students during recess as opposed to gym class. In gym class, students are given a game to play by a teacher that is structured by the teacher, explained by the teacher, and controlled by the teacher. While some students enjoy this, other students feel less engaged and exert less effort.

In contrast, when those same students are on the playground during recess, they regain a sense of control over their choice of what to play and how. In this situation, you can often observe a notable change in both effort and engagement. Students create elaborate imaginary games with rules, roles, and consequences *all on their own*! If you watch these games in action, you will notice that when given this independence, students rise to the occasion. The choices they make mean more to them since the game is *theirs*, therefore, they feel a greater desire to engage in that game with effort, self-discipline, and self-determination.

How to Introduce Independence Level Choices

The concept of Independence Level Choices must be discussed and taught directly before being implemented, just as the rebuilding area procedures or social skills instruction must be taught directly to students before being utilized. Begin by asking students what they think about when they hear the word "independent" and begin a discussion or word web. For younger students, you may want to simply compare an adult or "grown-up" to a child. Ask students how the two individuals are different? Your goal is to paint a picture comparing the fact that grown-ups or people who are acting independently do not need to *rely completely* on others to help them, guide them, or tell them what to do. Sure, this may be helpful at times, but generally people who are independent can control their own actions, make their own choices, and rely on themselves.

In contrast, ask students what they think about when they hear the word "dependent" and begin a discussion or word web. For younger students, bring them back to your comparison of a grown-ups as opposed to children. Ask students why children are sometimes dependent on the care of adults. What do they need adults to do for them, teach them, or help them with?

By the end of both discussions, have students make the letter "I" in sign language by making a fist and sticking out only their pinky finger. Have them place this "I" on their chest and sit up proudly as they repeat after you that this stands for the label **Independent**. Tell students that you will be using this word to describe students you see making independent choices in the classroom. Begin a discussion of what being independent looks like, sounds like, and feels like for several different times and places in your classroom (or whatever setting you wish).

Now hold up your "I" sign in front of you and use your other hand to make a letter "C." Have your students follow along using their hands. Explain that the capital "C" stands for **Coach**. Sometimes children and even adults need a coach to help them, guide them, or give them support when they do not know what to do or make a negative choice.

Now slowly move your two hands together and ask students what capital letter this looks like now? Explain that the letter "D" that they just made stands for **Dependent**. Tell students that you will be using this word to describe students you see who may need help or a "coach" (show your detached letter "C" again) to make better choices in the classroom. Begin a discussion of what being dependent looks like, sounds like and feels like for several different times and places in your classroom (or whatever setting you wish).

The main point to emphasize (and this is very easy to make visual using the hand gestures) is that at any given point a student can be in control of making an independent or dependent choice. You are using these terms to label their choices, *not* their identities. Make sure that you make this point clear. You may want to use an example connected to yourself such as, *"Even as an adult, I sometimes make **dependent** choices such as not paying my bills on time. When this happens, I get a consequence. That consequence is that I have to pay a late fee, which is more money than what I needed to pay if I had been more **independent** and remembered to pay my bill on time."* (Please visit website www.empowerprogram.net for a video demonstration).

How to Implement Independence Level Choices

This strategy can be implemented in a number of different ways, but all revolve around the common theme of having more or less choices based on the students' level of independence. Students who make independent choices and show independent behaviors can be afforded more choice. In comparison, students who make dependent choices and show dependent behaviors receive less choice. The types of choices you offer students is up to you as the educator, but it can be helpful to think about student choice from these three categories:

1. Privileges
2. Processes
3. Products

In terms of **privileges**, students who are showing independent level behavior may be afforded more choices such as being a special helper, leading a group, or doing an errand for a staff member that requires trust and responsibility. Students who are not acting as independently by comparison simply do not receive the same privileges.

In terms of **processes**, students who are showing independent level behavior may also enjoy having more choice over their typical classroom processes such as being able to choose where they do their work, what they use to do their work, or who they work with. Students who are not acting as independently by comparison may not earn such choices. Those students may instead have to do their work from an assigned space, using only given tools and working in pre-assigned groups or by themselves.

Finally, in terms of **products**, students who are showing independent level behavior may be given choices involving how they show what they know, or their learning products. This might look like having the choice to use multiple intelligences to create a project or other authentic product to show mastery of a lesson objective rather than completing a pre-assigned worksheet. The independent level students are still responsible for showing the same mastery of content as those students who are completing the assigned learning product, only they now have more control over how and what they use to do so.

In each example, the dependent level students are not being punished or treated unfairly. Those students merely do not have *as much choice* over their privilege, process, or product as those students who chose to show more independent behaviors. This is a great way to discuss the issue of consequences as simply the results of cause–effect relationships. When students cause a teacher to notice their level of independence by using their social skills and making positive choices, the effect is that they gain more choice. On the other hand, when students cause the teacher to notice their level of dependence by needing reminders to use their social skills or making negative choices, the effect is that they lose their chance to make their own choices and have to settle for someone else, such as the teacher, making their choices for them.

This small but mighty concept of independence level choices can have a huge effect on your students' sense of control over their classroom learning environment and also their relationship with you as the teacher. Instead of being viewed as judge, you are now simply the jury. You are not sentencing them with consequences, you are merely observing their choices and behaviors and providing them with the resulting options that they have earned based on the evidence provided. It is this transition of perceived control that can calm students' sense of fairness and reduce their need to engage in power struggles.

Strategy 3: Student Leadership

The final strategy in this section allows students to show independence and generosity while promoting pro-social behavior. By giving students avenues for developing leadership skills, they transition from being passive recipients of adult care to becoming caretakers themselves. This shift in role empowers young students to feel more in control of themselves and engages them in wanting to contribute to helping one another. The strategies below provide students with specific ways to develop those leadership skills.

Peer Coaching

The idea of introducing Peer Coaching is to promote students to use one another as resources for support, just as much as they would a teacher or other staff member. Offering students the option of acting as Peer Coaches for other students presents them with a chance to be independent, showing the skills they know, as well as generous by using those learned skills to help someone else. Peer coaching can be used for both academic and social situations.

Students tend to have strengths in one area, often balanced with weaknesses in another. For instance, a student that is extremely focused in class academically may lack that confidence in social scenarios. On the other hand, a student who is very confident socially may struggle with schoolwork. Of course this varies with each student, but Peer Coaching can present an opportunity for all students to use their individual strengths in order to support each other's weaknesses as a group.

To put this into a context that you can see, imagine a student who is very shy and doesn't stick up for themselves but always finishes their work and does so very accurately. That student could benefit from having the support of a Peer Coach when it comes to using social skills like "Communicating Concerns" or "Expressing Frustration." A student who feels confident socially could present as the perfect Social Skills Peer Coach in this situation. That coach will gain a sense of independence and generosity by being able to help the first student through their learning process of becoming more confident socially.

On the flip side, the very same student who seems so confident socially may struggle academically. This presents a great opportunity for the first student to act as a Schoolwork Peer Coach by helping the other student to feel more confident tackling their academic work with support. This symbiotic relationship also offers a natural opportunity for bonding between students of varying personalities. As the teacher, your ability to facilitate opportunities for these mutually beneficial relationships to occur in your classroom helps to support both students in that moment of social or academic need, while preventing potential bullying due to differences in personality or skills down the road.

How to Implement Peer Coaching

In order to actively implement this student leadership strategy, introduce Peer Coaching as a way for any student to take a leadership role in the classroom. It is critical that this role of Peer Coach be offered to anyone who would like to try and help his or her peers. This does not mean that if a student is not following directions or engaging in negative behaviors, he/she should be chosen as a Peer Coach at that time. However, the option needs to be available according to their behavior, just as with the strategy of Independence Level Choices. When the option is always available based on a student's own choices, that student becomes more motivated to strive for, rather than become daunted by, this opportunity.

Explain to your students that being a Peer Coach means you are able to show what you know about social skills or schoolwork (hinting that students must *act* the part in order to *get* the part). Explain that this is a form of leadership because now they are using what they know to help others as well as themselves. This makes them excellent leaders!

Discuss with students what the term "coach" means? Ask questions such as, "Does a coach do things *for* you?" Make this visual for students by asking about a baseball coach, for example. Ask students if the coach is on the field catching the ball for the first baseman during the game. Continue the discussion to engage students in delineating how the coach helps his team learn, but does not do things for them during the big game. Ask questions about what makes a good coach and let the students develop their own definition of what good coaching looks like, sounds like, and feels like. Making a chart of these answers is a great idea and can also present a nice visual reminder for what peer coaching should look like, sound like, and feel like for future reference.

Finally, take time to role-play (just as you would when teaching social skills) some scenarios with your students of how peer coaching might look in the context of your classroom. Practice modeling what helping rather than doing the work for someone looks like for schoolwork scenarios. Practice modeling what supporting rather than directing looks like for social skills scenarios. These skits can be incredibly helpful in clarifying this student leadership strategy for students. You may need to revisit modeling these scenarios throughout the year.

THE COMMUNICATION SPOT

An incredibly helpful support for social skills peer coaching is to create a physical Communication Spot in your classroom. Much like the Rebuilding Area, providing a concrete space to do the work of coaching—similar to a basketball court for an athlete or an office for a professional—makes it feel more serious for students.

To create a Communication Spot use colored duct tape or masking tape to make a large box on the carpet of floor in a determined area of your classroom. Then mark off a spot for each student to stand, facing each other. You can be creative and allow students to vote on their favorite sneakers, print a picture of two pairs, laminate and tape those to the floor with packing tape, or simply mark the two spots with a line of duct tape. You can then write the steps to the social skill "Communicating Concerns" directly on the duct tape to act as a script for students using the spot, or for the Peer Coach to use.

Have the Peer Coach practice standing outside the box as they support the other two students who are communicating with each other. This both reminds the coach that they are supporting not directing, and allows the students inside the Communication Spot to remember that they are the ones responsible for communicating with each other, even if the coach is helping to guide/mediate the process.

Student Think Tanks

Another effective process/strategy for promoting student leadership as well as positive classroom climate is introducing the use of Student Think Tanks. The concept of a think tank is defined as "a body of experts providing advice and ideas on specific political or economic problems." The power of introducing this idea to your younger students is to remind them that they can be a body of experts and can provide each other with advice or ideas on specific problems that exist within their classroom community. For younger students, the thought of "being an expert" or "giving advice" seems to be reserved for teachers and staff. Offering this option for students themselves is empowering and motivating while providing a natural stage for problem solving and self-discipline.

How to Introduce Student Think Tanks

When introducing this tool, show students a quick video of an adult think tank at work. You can look up any example ranging from famous multimillion dollar businesses or cutting edge nonprofit organizations fighting for social justice. Regardless, allow students to see and hear these adults working together, sharing ideas, listening to each other and moving forward towards making communal decisions. Discuss what students thought about what they saw? Did they think those adults were smart? What about how they used social skills? After showing this visual, empower students by offering them the opportunity to learn how to do the very same thing!

Engaging Students in Think Tanks

One option for engaging students in Think Tanks is to use large-scale or community-based problems. This works very well to spark their interest since the issues being discussed feel farther away from the students' common experience and thus seem more intriguing. Starting from this perspective can also help students to disengage from their preconceived roles in the classroom.

Students who may feel nervous about discussing something that they are directly involved in everyday in the classroom can be relieved of that stress when discussing an issue happening half a world away. This sense of detachment can fuel creativity, eliminate bias and promote more collective problem solving simply by removing the stress of discussing something that is closely connected with their immediate experience in the classroom.

When students come together to work towards an idea to solve a problem affecting the world or their larger community, they can all galvanize towards a common goal. Much like on the playground, when students have a common imaginary enemy, they tend to throw classroom tiffs aside in order to work as a team to defeat the "bad guy" or accomplish some other collective goal. Utilizing this mindset works beautifully when beginning the process of practicing working together in a Student Think Tank and can pave the way for students to use the very same collective skills to then transition into discussions about classroom problems later.

How to Implement Student Think Tanks

The actual implementation of Student Think Tanks is completely up to you. As the teacher, however, here are some helpful suggestions. Use Student Think Tanks when a classroom problem has been persisting, when students seem to be very resistant to something as a group, or when there are bullying concerns as a group. Regardless of the initial reason, make sure to structure your Student Think Tank time with the following musts:

1. Set ground rules as a group
2. Use a talking piece
3. Allow students to *run* the group, with you as the teacher *facilitating*

In order to set ground rules for the Student Think Tank time, invite your students to discuss what they remember seeing from the video of adult think tanks. Write a short list of things that made the group run well and then an opposing list of things that students feel would slow the group down. You can color code these in green and red to help orient students. After this discussion, ask students to submit their ideas on no more than three ground rules for Student Think Tank time and take a vote.

For a talking piece, any object will do. Some examples that have worked well: small stuffed animal, a ball, or a fake microphone. You can also choose to use an item that specifically relates to the topic being discussed to both engage and remind students of the focus of the group. For example, if you are discussing pollution in the community, you can pass around an empty plastic soda bottle. You can also use the same idea to focus a classroom community discussion by writing the topic, for example bullying, on a sticky note and taping that note to a small ball. If students go off topic, simply remind them to look at the "focus ball" or talking piece to remind them what they are to be focusing their talk time on.

Finally, remind yourself that you are not the teacher and director of this activity, but the facilitator. Your job, just like that of a Peer Coach, is to guide and support your students in their discussion, but not to *lead* that discussion. Student Think Tanks are just as much about teaching students to navigate the process of group problem solving and conversation as they are about actually solving the problem up for discussion. Therefore, as difficult as it may seem, allow moments of frustration and disagreement to occur. Allow students to pose suggestions on how to work through those times and then congratulate them when they do so successfully.

The genuine feeling of having worked through a problem situation using their own ideas, as opposed to being told what to do and how to do it by the teacher, is incredibly powerful for students. This can mean the difference between them feeling a sense of independence and wanting to engage in Student Think Tanks as a resource for problem solving in the future or feeling like this is yet another boring activity they are forced to participate in.

APPENDIX A

ENVIRONMENT P.O.P. RESOURCES

Learn Your ABCs Glossary

A - astute, adept, astonishing, alert, awesome, alarming, awe-inspiring, abundant, ample, apt, ambitious

B - bright, brilliant, bold, brainy, beautiful, breathtaking, big, big-league, best

C - clever, crafty, considerable, colossal, creative, calculated, capable, comprehensive

D - dazzling, deep, dynamite

E - exceptional, excellent, effective, enormous, extreme, enlightened

F - fresh, fabulous, fantastic, first-class, fine

G - glorious, great, genius, grand, gigantic, groovy

H - huge, humongous

I - impressive, intelligent, ingenious, immense, imaginative, incredible

J - jumbo, joy

K - keen, knowledgeable

L - luminous, legendary, love

M - magnificent, majestic, mind-blowing, mammoth, major-league, mondo, marvelous, monumental

N - nimble, numerous, noble

O - on the ball, original, outrageous, out of this world

P - perceptive, profound, phenomenal, peachy, primo

Q - quick, quirky, quality

R - remarkable, resourceful, ready, responsible, rad, rich

S - splendid, shining, smart, superb, sparkling, sharp, super, shrewd, slick, sassy, sublime, spectacular, stunning, striking, strong, stupendous

T - tremendous, titanic, towering, together, terrific

U - unbelievable, unconventional

V - vivid, vast

W - wise, whiz, wonderful, wondrous, witty

X

Y - yowza (complimentary statement of positive reaction)

Z - zealous

The Empower Program   *Environment Module*   **P.O.P Resource 2**

Correct and Connect Redirection Glossary

Problem Behavior	Social Skill Connection	Correct and Connect Redirection CORRECT – CONNECT *Italics used for specific social skills language prompts*
Yelling Rude Tone	Tone of Voice	"I need you to lower your volume – so I can help you?" "Can you change your tone please – so that your friend will want to listen to what you have to say?"
Sticking Tongue Out	Facial Expression	"Can you put your tongue back in your mouth please – and use it to ask for what you need instead?"
Head Down	Body Position	"I need you to lift your head please – so I can see your handsome/pretty face."
Too Close	Personal Space	"Can you give me some personal space please – so that everyone else can follow your excellent example!"
Tugging on Your Shirt for Attention	Communication	"Try raising your hand instead – I really want to be able to help you!"
Balling Up Fists	Keeping Your Cool	"Can you make a *mad meatball* instead – so you can get your anger out and make a great choice?"
Off Task	Time and Place	"I need you to put that away now – so that you can use it later when it's [insert alternative time or place] time instead!"
Whining While Waiting	Patience	"I bet you can *shrink and squash* # times while you wait – save your voice for the playtime you'll earn later by waiting now!"
Running Up To You (instead of raising hand)	Asking for Attention	"Show me another way to get my attention (pantomime raising your hand) – because I would love to help you!"
Eyes Wandering	Listening Position	"Let me see your faces – I want to remember what the next great [insert exciting job relating to what they are learning] look like for when you become famous later in your lives!"
Throwing Object	Handling Frustration	"Can you use your hands to raise for help instead of throwing that – I know you may be feeling upset and I want to help you."
Calling a Peer a Name	Communicating Frustration	"Can you use an I-statement instead of calling him a name – I want him to understand why he made you mad so we can fix it"
Arguing Over Consequence	Moving On	"Lets *blast the past and open the present* – so you can get back on track! I miss your excellent ideas in my group!"
Agonizing over Consequence (Pre-Tantrum)	Accepting Consequences	"I can see that you're feeling sad – let's *mind hop* and think about what could happen later when you move on like I know you can!"
Arguing with Another Student	Respectfully Disagreeing	"Can you show me how you can respectfully disagree? – You don't have to agree with each other but show me that how to do that using your smarty-pants social skills!"
Tattle Tailing	Communicating Concerns	"Can you *communicate your concern* to your friend so they understand by saying, *"Excuse me, I have a concern?"* – that would be a great way to handle this!"
Fighting Over Something	Problem Solving	"I bet you could show great problem-solving here – what smart ideas could you both think of without even needing my help?
Fighting Over Who Goes First	Choosing Who Goes First	"Try rock-paper-scissor or flipping a coin to decide – so you social skills leaders can get started!"
Problems Working in a Group	Strategies for Group Work	"Let's use the *circle strategy* from our social skill – so everyone has a job and gets a turn!"
Distracted	Finding Focus	"Use our Finding Focus song (pantomime *"heads, shoulders, eyes and ears"* motions) – so you can tell me where you are feeling distracted and we can get you back on track!"

The Empower Program   *Environment Module*   **P.O.P Resource 3**

Executive Questioning Help Sheet

Instead of saying, *"Why did you . . . "*

TRY . . .   **Executive Questioning Prompt**

WHAT   "What could you do to ask for help?"

"What do you think would be a better choice?

"What part of what you just did wasn't safe?"

"What other choice do you have now?"

"What time and place would be better for that choice?"

"What way could you help yourself now?"

"What do you think you can do?"

"What do you need right now?"

WHERE   "Where can you go when you need that?"

"Where do we put that when we are done with it?"

"Where is a better place to _____"

"Where do you know we can use that later?"

"Where would you like to go instead?"

"Where is your plan going to take place?"

"Where do you need to go now to fix it?"

HOW   "How can you make this better?"

"How do you think they are feeling?"

"How did that make them feel?"

"How do you think you can help yourself here?"

"How can you work this out?"

"How can you ask for help?"

"How else could you show me you know that?"

"How much time do you need to calm down?"

"How can I help you?"

"How can you show me you know how to do that?"

WHEN   "When do you think is a better time and place to do that?"

"When does your brain tell you would be a good time to ask for that?"

"When could you use that again?"

"When do you want to do that instead?"

"When are you going to let me know your choice?"

"When can you talk to him or her about this?"

The Empower Program   *Environment Module*   **P.O.P Resource 4**

Rebuilding Area Making Suggestion Sheet

Materials Check List for PICTURE RBA (pick and choose!)

- ❑ Pictures of students modeling each green, yellow or red choice (or board-maker/clip art)
- ❑ Pictures of feelings faces
  **(You can also use the *REBUILD* Solution Sheet for picture prompts)
- ❑ Possibly green, yellow and red paper
- ❑ Cardboard or Project Tri-Fold Board for base
- ❑ Velcro
- ❑ Laminating Machine for cards (or packing tape ☺)
- ❑ Area to designate for this space in classroom (or can use fold up board to be mobile)
- ❑ Marker to add sections and prompts

Materials Check List for DRY-ERASE RBA (pick and choose!)

- ❑ Pictures of students modeling each green, yellow or red choices (or board-maker/clip art)
- ❑ Pictures of feelings faces
  **(You can also use the *REBUILD* Solution Sheet for picture prompts)
- ❑ Packing Tape (or lamination)
- ❑ Board to mount your master RBA on (or binder cover/clipboard, etc.)
- ❑ Markers to add sections and prompts

Suggestions for Card Pictures

FEELINGS cards: sad, mad, excited, frustrated, confused, scared, worried, bored

RED cards: hitting, kicking, pushing, bullying, unsafe play, screaming, throwing object, leaving classroom without permission, etc.

YELLOW cards: calling out, unkind words, not following directions, distracted, not classroom supplies properly, making noises, etc.

GREEN cards: calm tone, calm face, calm body, raise my hand, talk it out, listen, use kind words, ask for space, walking feet, keep personal space, etc.

Suggestions for Processing Prompts

I am feeling _____. I chose to _____. Next time, I will choose to _____

I felt _____. My red or yellow choice was to _____. A green choice would be to _____.

I feel _____. I chose to _____. I can use my social skills to choose _____ next time!

 **EMPOWER Program**

Date: _____

Name: _____

1

VENT

How can I calm down?

I feel...

excited

mad

frustrated

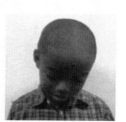

sad

confused

scared

worried

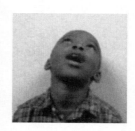

bored

What happened?

My picture of what happened

What can I do to help myself?

Raise my hand to ask

Listen again

Talk it out

Make a mad meatball

Ask for space to take a break

Tell the teacher

Use a SOCIAL SKILL I learned!

Date: _____

Name: _____

2

RENT

How can I ask for space?

			✓ Check it off
#1	Raise my hand		☐
#2	Ask for space to calm down		☐
#3	Teacher signs where you can have space	Where: _____ Teacher initial: _____	☐

The **EMPOWER Program**

Date: _____

Name: _____

3

REBUILD

How can I rebuild my choice?

What happened?

1st   **2nd**   **3rd**

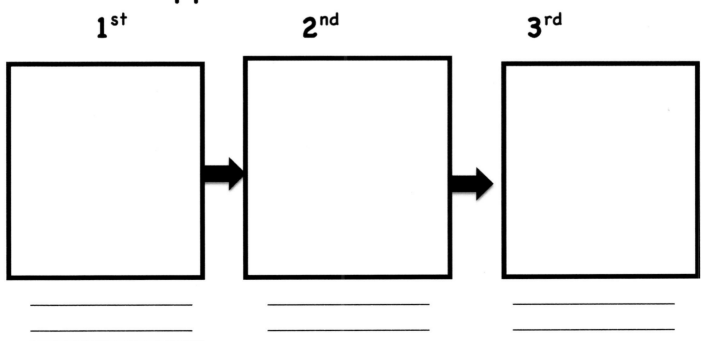

_____   _____   _____
_____   _____   _____

I felt...

mad

excited

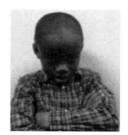

frustrated

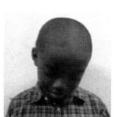

sad

confused

scared

worried

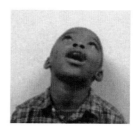

bored

My RED choice was...

push

scream

kick

hit

unsafe
body

leaving classroom
without permission

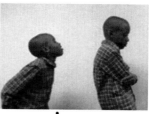

extreme
disrespect

1. Identify the problem

I felt

_____

- -

_____

I chose to

_____

- -

_____

because

_____

- -

_____

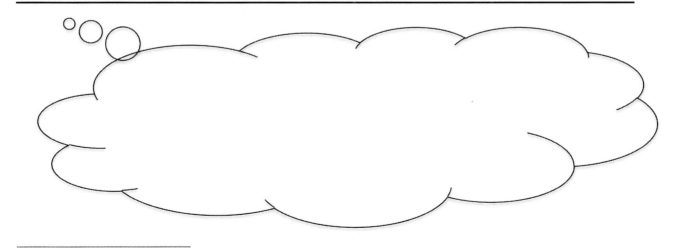

2. Think about the problem

Me	Them

My choice made <u>me</u>
think...

My choice made <u>them</u>

think...

3. Build a solution

What can I do to rebuild a better choice next time?

calm tone

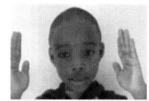

calm face

calm body

listen

raise my hand

sitting up

do my work

talk it out

ask for space

Use a SOCIAL SKILL I learned!

I can

_____

- -

_____

SOLUTION ACTION PLAN

Draw a picture of YOU putting your solution in ACTION!

Draw a picture of your RED choice **Instead of...**	Draw a picture of your GREEN choice, your SOLUTION! **I am now going to...**

Did I do it?
How many times can I show this solution in ACTION (use check marks or happy faces ☺)

I am ready to come back and be the best I can be!

_____   _____
                My Name   **Teacher**

The EMPOWER Program

Date: _____

Name:
_____
- -
_____ _____

4

RESPOND

How can I solve a conflict?

Choose how you want to RESPOND instead of REACT below:

➡️ CONFRONT   ❓ QUESTION   🗨️ REPORT

(Use this sheet and the back to help you practice and plan!)

CONFRONT		
1.	Use a calm but <u>confident</u> <u>tone</u> of voice	
2.	Use an I-statement to <u>communicate</u> how you felt ➡️ *"I felt _____ when you _____."*	*I felt —*
3.	Use a <u>confronting</u> statement to tell them what you need ➡️ *"I need you to _____."*	

QUESTION

1.	Use a calm but <u>confident</u> <u>tone</u> of voice	
2.	<u>Ask</u> the person <u>why</u> they did what they did? *"Why did you do that?"*	
3.	<u>Listen</u> to what they have to say <u>Repeat</u> what they said *"I heard you say _____"* <u>Respond</u> to them *"I need you to _____"*	

REPORT

1.	Write or draw what happened below: Who was there: _____ What happened: _____ My picture of what happened:	
2.	Find a helping adult to show your report to and ask for help	

APPENDIX B

ABILITY P.O.P RESOURCES

The Empower Program   *Ability Module*   **P.O.P Resource 1**

Common Language Prompts Sheet

Social Skill	Common Language Prompt for PRAISE	Common Language Prompt for REDIRECTION
Tone of Voice	*"I loved your low **tone of voice** when you asked for that. I would be glad to get it for you!"*	*"Can you please adjust your **tone of voice** to a calm one and ask me again?"*
Facial Expression	*"Wow, your **facial expression** really says you are listening and ready to go!"*	*"Can you check your **facial expression**? I think it might be telling your friend something that is making them upset . . . "*
Body Position	*"By looking at [student's name] **body position**, I can see that he is ready to try."*	*"You are so close to being ready, just look at your **body position**. Can you bring your head up so you can look like the leader I know you are?"*
Personal Space	*"Beautiful! [Student] is showing exactly how to get in line and leave **personal space**. Who else can show me that?"*	*"I love the way you got in line so quickly, can you show me some more **personal space**?"*
Communication	*"[Student], not only did you stay calm, but I love the way you chose to **communicate** your concern instead of yelling. Are you sure you're not an 8th grader?"*	*"Can you **communicate** with her using an I-statement instead of yelling?"*
Keeping Your Cool	*"The way you just **kept your cool** shows me that you are really working on controlling your anger. I am really proud of you for that!"*	*"I know that you are mad, try **keeping your cool** so that I can help you instead of you getting in trouble. Start by making a **mad meatball**, remember?"*
Time and Place	*"I really like the way [student] chose to wait to run until she got to the playground. That was the perfect **time and place** for running!"*	*"I know that you want to play with your toy right now but it's just not the right **time and place**. Can you tell me by looking at our schedule what **time and place** you CAN play with it?"*
Patience	*"Look at the **patience** [student] is showing by **shrinking and squashing** while she waits. What a smart way to wait!"*	*"I can see that you want it now, try practicing our **patience** social skill by using your hands to **shrink and squash** 10 times. By then, it may just be your turn!"*
Asking for Attention	*"I love the way that [student] just **asked for attention** by raising his hand."*	*"Hmmm, I bet you can think of another way to **ask for my attention** besides calling out. I wonder **H.O.W**"* (pantomime hand and on paper choices)
Listening Position	*"Look at [student's name] **listening position**! What a pro! He is 4 for 4: Head up, voice off, body calm, AND eyes on. Woah!"*	*"Can you help our friend by silently modeling the one part of her **listening position** I need her to show me? She is almost there! Who can help her?"*
Handling Frustration	*"I saw that! The way you just used your hand to make that **mad meatball** to **handle your frustration** . . . I should call the Awesome Police!"*	*"I can see you're frustrated. You can **handle your frustration** by using our social skill! Remember we learned 4 different ways with our hands?"*
Communicating Frustration	*"I like the way you said **Excuse Me** to let her know you wanted to **communicate your frustration**. That must have been really hard since you are mad, but you did it. Good job! Keep going . . . "*	*"Freeze! This is a perfect time to **communicate your frustration**. Start by saying **Excuse me** and let me know if you need more help!"*

Social Skill	Common Language Prompt for PRAISE	Common Language Prompt for REDIRECTION
Moving On	*"I have to say . . . you might be the best past blaster I've ever seen! You could have stayed stuck in that bad mood all day but no, not my man. He just BOOM blasted the past and now you can open the present. Way to move on [student], great job!"*	*"This isn't the best news now, but let's try using our social skill moving on! Get your dynamite ready . . . BLAST the past, now you can open the present! If you move on now, what can we look forward to doing later?"*
Accepting Consequences	*"Did you just mind hop all by yourself? High five for that. What did you see happening if you accepted this consequence and moved on? Yup, I agree. Great choice!"*	*"I know that you don't like that but if you can accept your consequence I bet you can earn back your spot? Can you mind hop with me and imagine that instead of just being mad? Tell me how you would feel after you move on?"*
Respectfully Disagreeing	*"We have our first lawyer, ladies and gentleman! She could have acted like a little kid here but nope, she respectfully disagreed instead and kept her cool."*	*"Can I interrupt your disagreement for just one second please? You guys realize you don't have to agree on this? You can respectfully disagree and then choose another activity instead of fighting and losing playtime altogether. Does that make sense?"*
Communicating Concerns	*[Staring in awe . . .] "Would you two mind showing the principal how you just communicated your concern with each other? She would be so proud to see this! We may also need to write a good note home, too, you guys just did such a good job."*	*"Rewind real quick . . . (Pantomime weird rewinding noise) Okay—show me how you can communicate your concern instead of yelling at each other. Do you remember the first step?"*
Problem Solving	*"Ooh I have some problem solving artists in this classroom! Look at this amazing picture, and they circled the part they want help with . . . LOVE IT!"*	*"This sounds like a problem . . . WAIT, I know – we could use our problem solving social skill to help! Try drawing a picture of the problem and see if you can circle the part that needs fixing? I'll check back soon!"*
Choosing Who Goes First	*"Just saw a group using rock-paper-scissor to choose who goes first. Got a lot of social skills love for that group showing us how it's done without needing a teacher to help."*	*"Why don't you guys use one of our choosing who goes first strategies? Would you like a coin or would you like to play rock-paper-scissor?"*
Identifying Goals	*"I spy someone with GREAT social skills! [Student] was able to identify his goal for reading group today without even needing my help."*	*"Instead of having to listen to me tell you what to do, I bet you can identify your own goal for group today! Try drawing a picture of what you want to learn by the end of this group then see if you can put it into words?"*
Breaking Down Big Goals	*"Someone knows how to make a pizza pie to break down this big goal! He even has 2 steps written already. I can't even keep up!"*	*"It seems like so much right now. We may want to take a break and make a pizza pie. Can you remember how we can use a pizza pie to help us break down this big goal?"*
Strategies to Reach Your Goal	*"Nouns, nouns, nouns! This young lady has decided to use her folder as a tool to help her concentrate on reading. That was super creative. Way to strategize, my friend!*	*"Can you think of some nouns you might use to help you reach your goal? What person, place or thing could help?"*
Strategies for Group Work	*"I see an awesome circle going on in this group! I didn't even need to remind them that they are using our social skill of group work strategies. How independent!"*	*"I can see that you guys are a little stuck. Why don't you use our group work strategy of making a job circle to try and help?"*
Finding Focus	*"Thank you so much for telling me that the cars outside were distracting you. I can move your seat over here. Great job finding your focus!"*	*"I can see that something is stealing your focus away from us. Can you use our finding focus song to help you tell me what it is?"*

Master Teacher Lesson Frame

Skill Set:

Grade Range:

Social Skill:

Common Core Standard Link:

Materials:

Objective:

Hook

Create an experience:

Analyze the experience:

Teach

Define the skill:

Identify the Skill Steps: *(See* Student Social Skills Cards *for skill steps)*

Practice

Perform

The Empower Program   *Ability Module*   **P.O.P Resource 3**

Weekly Framework for Instructional Activities Grid

DAY (ORDER) WHAT *(Level of Blooms Taxonomy)* WHY	INSTRUCTIONAL ACTIVITY	BRIEF DESCRIPTION
Monday (Day 1) **Direct Instruction** *Knowledge Level* Teach students social skills content directly	Direct Instruction Lesson Plan	Use lesson plans in Appendix B
	Master Teacher Lesson Frame	Use "Master Teacher Lesson Frame" in Appendix B
Tuesday (Day 2) **Review Game** *Comprehension Level* Review basic steps of social skill in fun way	Basketball Review Game	Using a hoop or basket of some kind, have students shoot a basket for each skill step they remember correctly.
	Board Game Review	Create simple board game templates where students land on ACT IT OUT, SAY IT or DRAW IT for each skill step. Students play the board game to review the skill steps.
Wednesday (Day 3) **Steps in Stride** *Application Level* Engage students to contextualize social skills steps	Scenario Spin Bean Bag/Eraser Toss Fly Swatter Relay Race	Use a spinner, dice, bean bag, eraser or fly swatters to have students choose scenarios to act out the skill in context (examples and non-examples)
Thursday (Day 4) **Media Madness** *Analysis Level* Connect student interests with new social skills content	Cartoon Analysis Interview a TV Character	Play a clip of a high-interest cartoon and analyze that cartoon based on the social skills steps. Have students critique when the characters used or could have used the skill steps. You can also have students pretend to interview one of the TV characters after watching the clip to provide further analysis (and fun)
Friday (Day 5) **Portfolio Pages** *Synthesis and Evaluation Levels* Authentic Assessment	Linguistic	Write a poem or story
	Visual-Spatial	Draw a comic strip, poster or picture
	Bodily-Kinesthetic	Create a dance
	Logical-Mathematical	Compare/Contrast the steps
	Musical	Write a song or rap
	Interpersonal	Create a commercial with a group
	Intrapersonal	Write a journal entry about your experience
	Naturalist	Write/draw about relation to nature/ animals

SELF SKILL
TONE OF VOICE

The way your voice makes someone else feel

SKILL STEPS **VISUALS**

☐ **Stop and listen...**
How does my
voice sound?

☐ **Mind Movie**
How could my voice
make someone else feel?

☐ **Ask yourself...**
1. What do I want to happen?
2. How can I use my voice to help?

SELF SKILL
FACIAL EXPRESSION

What your face can "say" without your voice

SKILL STEPS **VISUALS**

☐ **Stop and look...**
How does my
face look?

☐ **Mind Movie**
How could the look on my
face make someone else feel?

☐ **Ask yourself...**
1. What do I want to happen?
2. How can I use my face to help

SELF SKILL
BODY POSITION

What your body can "say" without your voice

SKILL STEPS **VISUALS**

☐ **Stop and look...**
How does my body
position look?

☐ **Mind Movie**
How could my body position
make someone else feel?

☐ **Ask yourself...**
1. What do I want to happen?
2. How can I use my body position
to help?

SELF SKILL
PERSONAL SPACE

The safe space between you and someone else

SKILL STEPS

☐ **Stop and look...**
Where is my bubble?

☐ **Measure...**
Am I inside my bubble?

☐ **Ask yourself...**
1. Am I in someone else's bubble?
2. If I am, how can I fix that?

SELF SKILL
COMMUNICATION

How you let someone know what you need, want or feel

SKILL STEPS   **VISUALS**

☐ **Stop and think...**
**How does my
voice sound?**

☐ **Ask yourself H.O.W**

How can I let them know?

H - Raise my **hand** or use a signal

O - Write or draw it **on paper**

W - I can use my **words**

STOP SKILL
KEEPING YOUR COOL

How to calm down when you are upset

SKILL STEPS   **VISUALS**

☐ **Mad meatball!**
  ✓ **Staying in my bubble**
  ✓ **Squeezing my hands**

☐ **Count to 10**
Use my fingers

   1

☐ **Take a rising breath**
1. Breath in, rise up 1-2-3
2. Hold it 1-2-3
3. Let it out slow 1-2-3

   2

☐ **Use an "I-statement"**
to communicate   **3**

STOP SKILL
TIME AND PLACE

How to make good choices in different places

SKILL STEPS   **VISUALS**

☐ **Stop and think...**
**Right now I am at _____,
and it's time for _____.**

☐ **Mind Hop...**
"If I _____, _____ might happen..."

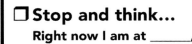

☐ **Make a green choice...**
"I can choose to _____!"

STOP SKILL
WAITING

How to help you wait

SKILL STEPS   **VISUALS**

☐ **Stop and check**
Am I in my bubble?

☐ **Shrink and Squash
the time as you WAIT!**
1. MATCH your finger buddies

2. SHRINK them together

3. SQUASH them tight

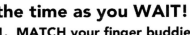

STOP SKILL
ASKING FOR ATTENTION

How to ask when you need attention

SKILL STEPS   **VISUALS**

☐ **Stop and think...**
**What is the TIME and
PLACE right now?**

☐ **Ask yourself H.O.W**
How can I ask for attention?

H - Raise my <u>hand</u> or use a signal

O - Write or draw it <u>on paper</u>

W - I can use my <u>words</u>

STOP SKILL
LISTENING POSITION

How to show someone you are ready and listening

SKILL STEPS   **VISUALS**

☐ **Head up**   ⬆

☐ **Voice off**   ✖

☐ **Body calm**

☐ **Eyes on**   ➡ ⬅

SIMMER SKILL
HANDLING FRUSTRATION

How to let out frustration in a positive way

SKILL STEPS   **VISUALS**

☐ **Stop and think**
Plan in my hand!

☐ <u>**HAND**</u>**ling this up or down:**

1. **Hand up to talk it out**

2. **Hand up to ask for space**

3. **Hand down to draw
   or write it out**

4. **Hand down to make a
   mad meatball**

SIMMER SKILL
COMMUNICATING FRUSTRATION

How to tell someone you are frustrated

SKILL STEPS   **VISUALS**

☐ **Stop and breathe...**

☐ **Use a calm tone**

☐ **Say, "Excuse me"**

☐ **Use an "I-statement"**
"I didn't like it when _____"
"I feel _____"
"I need you to _____"

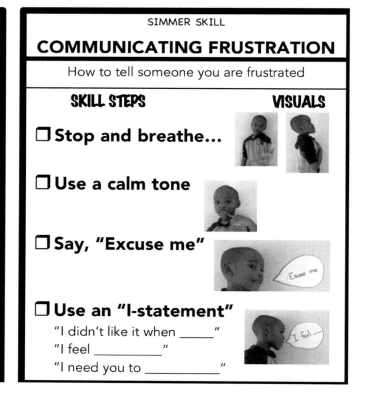

SIMMER SKILL
MOVING ON

How to move past a mistake

SKILL STEPS   **VISUALS**

☐ **Take a rising breath**

1   **2**   **3**

☐ **Think...**

Blast the PAST... Open the PRESENT!

☐ **Imagine your present**

SIMMER SKILL
ACCEPTING CONSEQUENCES

How to keep calm and handle a consequence

SKILL STEPS   **VISUALS**

☐ **Stop and squeeze**
Make a mad meatball

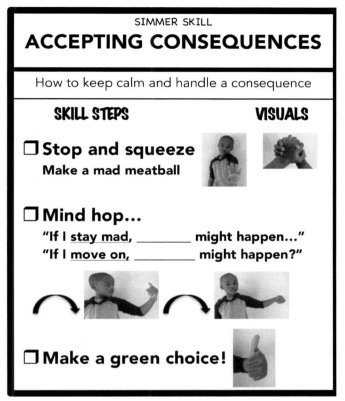

☐ **Mind hop...**
"If I <u>stay mad</u>, _____ might happen..."
"If I <u>move on</u>, _____ might happen?"

☐ **Make a green choice!**

SIMMER SKILL
RESPECTFULLY DISAGREEING

How to disagree in a respectful way

SKILL STEPS   **VISUALS**

☐ **Check your T.F.B**

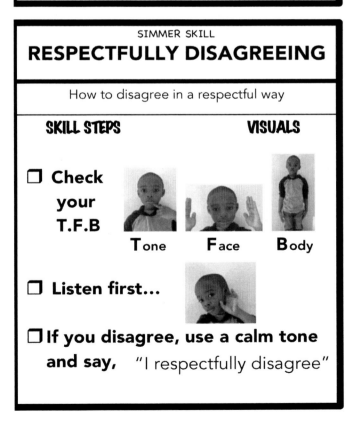

Tone   **F**ace   **B**ody

☐ **Listen first...**

☐ **If you disagree, use a calm tone and say,** "I respectfully disagree"

SOLVE SKILL
COMMUNICATING CONCERNS

How to tell someone when you have a problem

SKILL STEPS   **VISUALS**

☐ **Check Your T.F.B**

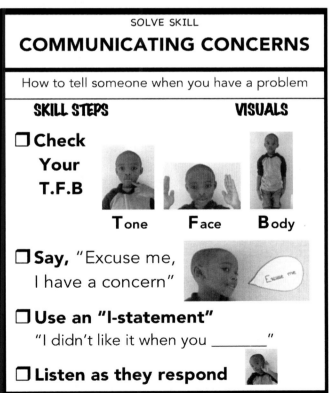

Tone   **F**ace   **B**ody

☐ **Say,** "Excuse me, I have a concern"

☐ **Use an "I-statement"**
"I didn't like it when you _____"

☐ **Listen as they respond**

SOLVE SKILL
JOINING A GROUP

How to ask to become part of a group

| **SKILL STEPS** | **VISUALS** |

☐ **Use a calm tone of voice**

☐ **Say,** "Excuse me, may I join you?"

☐ **Listen for the group to answer...**

☐ **Say,** "Thank you" **if they say YES**
Say, "OK" **if they say NO and move on to another choice**

SOLVE SKILL
COMPROMISE

How to find a solution that both people agree on

| **SKILL STEPS** | **VISUALS** |

☐ **Stop and think...**
How can we BOTH get what we want?

☐ **Listen to what they want**

☐ **Say what you want**

☐ **Talk about how you can agree, or try:**
1. Taking turns using a timer
2. Sharing or working together
3. Asking for help together

SOLVE SKILL
PROBLEM SOLVING

How to make a problem better

| **SKILL STEPS** | **VISUALS** |

☐ **Take a rising breath**
1   2   3

☐ **Make the problem a picture**

☐ **Circle the part you want to fix**

☐ **Pick a fix:**

Use a social skill **OR** Ask for help

SOLVE SKILL
CHOOSING WHO GOES FIRST

How to choose who goes first in a fair way

| **SKILL STEPS** | **VISUALS** |

☐ Pick a strategy:

1. Rock-Paper-Scissor
- Play Rock-Paper-Scissor 3 times
- The person who wins 2 goes first
- If it's a tie, shoot again

| <u>Paper</u> covers Rock | <u>Scissors</u> cut paper | <u>Rock</u> beats scissors |

2. Flip a coin
- One person flips, the other calls H or T
- The flipper is the other side of the coin
- Flip the coin 1 time

STRIVE SKILL
IDENTIFYING GOALS

How to set a goal for yourself

SKILL STEPS   **VISUALS**

☐ **Stop and think**
What to I want to do?

☐ **"Eye"-dentify with your eyes!**
Draw a picture of your goal.
What will it look like for you to get it?

☐ **Give it words**
Write or say,

"My goal is to _____"

STRIVE SKILL
BREAKING DOWN BIG GOALS

How to give your big goal little steps

SKILL STEPS   **VISUALS**

☐ **Stop and think**
Pizza pie!

☐ **Sort your ingredients**
Draw the things that you think
you need to make your goal...
(like ingredients in a pizza)

☐ **Write your recipe**
Make a list of 3 steps
that you think you need
to do to get to your goal

STRIVE SKILL
STRATEGIES TO REACH
YOUR GOALS

How to get to your goal

SKILL STEPS   **VISUALS**

☐ **Stop and think**
I need my NOUNS!

☐ **Choose your NOUNS:**
PERSON - Who **can I use to help me?**
PLACE - Where **is the best place?**
THINGS - What **can I use to help me?**

☐ **Ask your nouns for help!**
PEOPLE: Parents, Friends, Teachers, Coaches
PLACES: Special place or Special time
THINGS: Timer, Post-it note, Divider, Chart

STRIVE SKILL
STRATEGIES FOR WORKING
IN GROUPS

How to work with others to get to your goal

SKILL STEPS   **VISUALS**

☐ **Stop and think**
What is our goal?
Write it so everyone can see it

☐ **Ask each other...**
What jobs can we each do well?

Write/Build/Draw   Listen   Organize   Timer
(HANDS)   (EARS)   (EYES)   (MIND)

☐ **Use a circle to work as a team!**
Go in a circle as you work, giving people a
chance to do their job as you go around

STRIVE SKILL

FINDING FOCUS

How to find your focus when you are distracted

SKILL STEPS   **VISUALS**

☐ **Stop and think**
   Where in my body am I feeling distracted?

☐ **Use a song to find out where...**
   "Head...shoulders, eyes or ears?"

   HEAD – a worry?

   EYES – a thing you can see?

   EARS – a sound?

   SHOULDERS – a body feeling?

☐ **Tell someone** "I feel distracted from..."

SKILL STEPS   **VISUALS**

The Empower Program   **Lesson Plan 1**

Skill Set: Self-Skills

Grade Range: K-2

Social Skill: Tone of Voice

Big Picture Goal: Development of self-awareness skills

Common Core Standard Link: CCSS.ELA-LITERACY.CCRA.SL.1

Materials: Talking piece (optional), crayons (or other classroom prop)

Objective: Students will be able to perform, with a partner, the skill steps for *Tone of Voice*, using the skill card as a resource, and verbalizing how their tone makes someone else feel.

Hook

Create an experience: Tell students to close their eyes and pretend that they are in a jungle surrounded by tall, wet green grass. Tell them that the sun is beating down on their backs. Say that you hear something coming in the distance . . . what's that sound? *ROAR!* (Either give your best lion roar or play an audio clip). Ask students "How do you feel?" (Provide some suggestions of feelings and remind them to keep their eyes closed!) Ask them, "What do you want to do?" Ask them to identify what they think made that sound and why? Now say, "okay, we have escaped from the lion . . . phew that was close! Now what is that I hear? *MEOW* . . . (Either meow or play an audio clip). Ask the same three questions as before.

Analyze the experience: Now ask students to open their eyes and tell them how mean they are! Explain that you know the lion and the kitten very, very well and they were *both* just very sad because they had stepped on a thorn and it was stuck in their paw! Ask them why they were so mean to the lion and so kind to the kitten? Pass a ball or talking piece (or simply call on students) to share their ideas. The end goal is to discover with the students how they did *not* want to go anywhere near the lion, but how they felt sorry for the kitten **because of the tone of their voice!**

Teach

Define the skill: *The way your voice makes someone else feel.*

Identify the Skill Steps:

1. Stop and listen – How does my voice sound?

2. Mind Movie – How could my voice make someone else feel?

3. Ask yourself - 1. What do I want to happen?

          2. How can I use my tone of voice to help?

Use physical gestures to cue each skill step such as having students follow the leader as you use your hand to cue *"Stop"* (hand out) and *"Listen"* (hand touching ear). Invite students to watch a "mind movie" with you by pointing to your brain and looking up as you say, *"How could my voice make someone else feel?"* Then describe what you are seeing in your mind to illustrate this. Finally, let your students know that this last step is their chance to be in charge and ask themselves the above two questions instead of having a teacher or adult do it for them! Ask them how great it would feel to not have a teacher bossing you around? With each step, allow students the opportunity to discuss and make connections to their school, their community and themselves.

Practice

Guided Practice: In a whole group, provide a student with a tangible object, such as a crayon, and then model using an angry tone of voice to ask for the crayon. Have the students watching give you a thumb up or a thumb down. Next, ask the student you chose how they felt about the tone you used to ask. Now model asking in a calm tone of voice. Ask the class for thumbs up or down and again ask your partner how they felt and if it was different? Now brainstorm five situations where you could practice tone of voice using objects in the classroom and write them on the board. Suggestion: use situations that frequently occur in your classroom so that students can really contextualize!

Perform

Independent Practice: Pair students up or use small groups and have them practice using a calm tone of voice as well as a not-so-calm tone of voice with their partners using the practice situation. Give them several tangible materials to use as props to help guide their interaction.

The Empower Program   Lesson Plan 2

Skill Set: Self-Skills

Grade Range: K-2

Social Skill: Facial Expression

Big Picture Goal: Development of self-awareness skills

Common Core Standard Link: CCSS.ELA-LITERACY.CCRA.SL.1

Materials: Talking piece (optional), pictures of faces (optional), paper, crayons, mirrors (optional)

Objective: Students will be able to perform the skill steps for *Facial Expression*, using the skill card as a resource, after drawing their "happy/angry" face diagram.

Hook

Create an experience: Tell students that you are going to play a guessing game. You are going to make several different faces and they will tell you how they think you are feeling and what you may be thinking. Show pictures of or make (with your own face) a happy face, then a surprised face, a mad face, etc. Call on a student to come up and stand next to you as you pantomime thinking while the student acts as your speech bubble, saying what they think you are thinking (you may want to prep this student ahead of time).

Analyze the experience: Write the word term "Facial Expression" on the board. Pass a talking piece or ball around and ask students if they can find a small word inside those big words that reminds them of the guessing game? (You are looking to box FAC . . . and explain that "facial" means having to do with their face). Ask students what they think the word "expression" means? After collecting several ideas, explain that it means the act of showing your feelings. Show that you can "express" yourself in many ways (words, drawings, dancing . . . and with your face!)

Teach

Define the skill: *Facial expression is what your face "says" without your voice.*

Identify the Skill Steps:

1. Stop and look – How does my face look?
2. Mind Movie – How could the look on my face make someone else feel?
3. Ask yourself – 1. What do I want to happen?

    2. How can I use my facial expression to help?

Use physical gestures to cue each skill step such as having students follow the leader as you use your hand to cue *"Stop"* (hand out) and *"Look"* (pointing to your eyes). Invite students to watch a "mind movie" (a kid-friendly term for "visualize") with you by pointing to your brain and looking up as you say, *"How could the look on my face make someone else feel?"* Then describe what you are seeing in your mind to illustrate this. Finally, let your students know that this last step is their chance to be in charge of their own behavior by asking *themselves* the above two questions instead of having a teacher or adult do it for them! With each step, allow students the opportunity to discuss and make connections to their school, their community and themselves.

Practice

Guided Practice: Demonstrate drawing a diagram of your blank face. Draw an oval with a line splitting your face vertically down the middle. You can choose to have the students do this with you on their own diagrams or model and then have them finish by themselves. Start by labeling one side "HAPPY" and the other side "ANGRY." Now ask a student to come up and model a happy face and call on students to observe how their eyes, cheeks, nose and mouth look. Draw this on the diagram. Now have the student model an angry face. Students observe the differences in that student's eyes, cheeks, nose and mouth and draw these on the opposite side of the diagram. Show an example with one of the above comparisons before students break out to create their own diagrams (ex. Slanted eyebrow over eye vs. raised eyebrow).

Perform

Independent Practice: Have students create their own facial expression diagrams either using mirrors or a partner as a model. When students are finished, have them use another color to label each part of their diagram with how it might make the other person feel (connecting to skill step 2). To connect to step 3, ask students which side of the diagram looks like someone who you might want to help when they need something and why?

The Empower Program   Lesson Plan 3

Skill Set: Self-Skills

Grade Range: K-2

Social Skill: Body Position

Big Picture Goal: Development of self-awareness skills

Common Core Standard Link: CCSS.ELA-LITERACY.CCRA.SL.1

Materials: Talking piece (optional), book, crayons, paper

Objective: Students will be able to perform the skill steps for *Body Position*, using the skill card as a resource, by creating a drawing independently or acting it out with a partner.

Hook

Create an experience: Have students come to the rug or make a circle with their chairs and say you will be sharing a story with them. Get a book and find the farthest corner of the room, away from your students, and crouch down, facing away and begin reading story. After you are finished, or as soon as a student notices your inappropriate body position for shared reading, come back the group and begin to analyze.

Analyze the experience: Use a ball or talking piece to facilitate a conversation about your choice of body position when reading the story. Ask students, "How did it make you feel?"

Teach

Define the skill: *Body position is what your body can "say" without your voice.*

Identify the Skill Steps:

1. Stop and look – How does my body position look?

2. Mind Movie – How could my body position make someone else feel?

3. Ask yourself – 1. What do I want to happen?

                    2. How can I use my body position to help?

Use physical gestures to cue each skill step such as having students follow the leader as you use your hand to cue *"Stop"* (hand out) and *"Look"* (pointing to your eyes). Invite students to watch a "mind movie" with you by pointing to your brain and looking up as you say, *"How could my body position make someone else feel?"* Then describe what you are seeing in your mind to illustrate this. Finally, let your students know that this last step is their chance to be in charge and ask themselves the above two questions instead of having a teacher or adult do it for them! With each step, allow students the opportunity to discuss and make connections to their school, their community and themselves.

Practice

Guided Practice: Explain to students that they will be practicing this skill by either drawing pictures of their own or using their bodies to act it out in pairs. Write the following three words on the board: SLEEPING, LISTENING, and EATING. Tell students that you are going to act out, using your body, what your body position should look like when doing those three activities as well as a non-example of what your body should not look like. Call on a student to be your partner and as you act each activity out, ask your partner to tell you and the class what they think of your examples and non-examples. Now model the drawing choice by drawing an example and non-example picture of what you think your body position should or should not look like under each of the words. Ask students to raise their hands to tell you something they notice about your pictures.

Perform

Independent Practice: Allow students to choose which activity they would like to use for practice and send them on their way! Be sure to circulate, asking facilitating questions such as "What do you notice about how he/she is standing?" or "Why did you draw that person doing that?"

The Empower Program   Lesson Plan 4

Skill Set: Self-Skills

Grade Range: K-2

Social Skill: Personal Space

Big Picture Goal: Development of self-awareness skills

Common Core Standard Link: CCSS.ELA-LITERACY.CCRA.SL.1

Materials: Talking piece (optional), tape, post-it-notes, index cards

Objective: Students will be able to perform the skill steps for *Personal Space*, in a small group using the skill card as a resource, demonstrating their space using their "bubble."

Hook

Create an experience: Begin by placing small pieces of masking tape (or another visual indicator) extremely close together in a line on the floor. Ask several students to come up and stand on each spot in line (they should be over-crowded and almost unable to balance standing up because they are so close). When students begin to fall down or look uncomfortable, appear confused and ask, "What's the matter?" Have the group go back to their seats and begin the discussion on the importance of personal space.

Analyze the experience: Use a ball or talking piece to pass around as you call on students for their feedback about your line spots. You are eliciting feedback about the lack of personal space that you didn't leave room for when you laid out the spot markers. Ask, "Why is it important to have personal space between you and someone else?" "Do you think personal space can be different for different people?" "Is your personal space different for the people in your family than it would be for a stranger?"

Teach

Define the skill: *The safe space between you and someone else.*

Identify the Skill Steps:

1. Stop and look – Where is my bubble?

2. Measure – Am I inside my bubble?

3. Ask yourself – 1. Am I in someone else's bubble?

      2. If I am, how can I fix that?

Use your arms to form a circle in front of your body, almost as if your belly had grown to the maximum size and you were hugging it. This is the gestural prompt your students can use to measure their own personal space, as well as measure their distance from someone else. Use physical gestures to cue each skill step such as having students follow the leader as you use your hand to cue *"Stop"* (hand out) and *"Look"* (pointing to eyes) for the "bubble" idea. Finally, let your students know that this last step is their chance to be their own boss and ask themselves the above two questions instead of having a teacher or adult do it for them! With each step, allow students the opportunity to discuss and make connections to their school, their community and themselves.

Practice

Guided Practice: Give students the chance to re-do your lining up experiment, but using the new information they just learned about "Personal Space." Ask guiding questions such as, *"What would you do differently?"* or *"If you were the teacher, how would you ask your students to line up so that they had enough personal space?"* Invite a new group of students up to line up and one student to lead them.

Perform

Independent Practice: Divide the class into small groups and have them practice measuring their personal space using their bubbles. For some groups, challenge them by giving them different scenarios such as, *"What would you do if you were to going up to someone to say hello?"* *"What might your personal space look like then?"* Have students come up with 3-5 times where personal space would be important to use and model for the class.

The Empower Program   Lesson Plan 5

Skill Set: Self-Skills

Grade Range: K-2

Social Skill: Communication

Big Picture Goal: Development of self-awareness skills

Common Core Standard Link: CCSS.ELA-LITERACY.CCRA.SL.1

Materials: Talking piece (optional), crayons, markers, paper, felt ball

Objective: Students will be able to perform the skill steps for *Communication* by creating and sharing posters with drawings including the "H.O.W" strategy.

Hook

Create an experience: Gather your class and explain that you will be playing a couple of short games to start the lesson. First introduce the game of charades and quickly remind them that in this game, the actors cannot use words but must act out what they want the rest of the class to guess. Call on a student to come up and be the actor and whisper something in his/her ear to act out. Now introduce a second guessing game, Pictionary! Explain that you will call on a second student to come up to the board and they will have two minutes to draw what they want us to guess! Call on a student, whisper your direction and have them draw as classmates guess. Finally, explain the game "Can You Guess That Word" and call on two students to come up and play. Write down a word you want them to guess on a piece of paper in large lettering and ask the other student to close their eyes. Show that students' partner, as well as the rest of the class and then set the timer for two minutes and have the partner begin giving them verbal clues to guess the word.

Analyze the experience: Explain that all three of these games used the same concept in three different ways. They all involved "Communication." Ask students how they observed that they communicated differently in each game (Charades = body language and non-verbal, Pictionary = using pictures and your hands, and "Can You Guess That Word" = using words). Also mention that communication is not just using spoken words, as they just found out.

Teach

Define the skill: *How you let someone know what you need, want or feel.*

Identify the Skill Steps:

1. Stop and think – How does my voice sound?

2. Ask yourself – H.O.W can I let them know?

> **H** – Raise my <u>hand</u> or use a signal
>
> **O** – Write or draw it <u>on paper</u>
>
> **W** – I can use my <u>words</u>

Use physical gestures to cue each skill step such as having students follow the leader as you use your hand to cue *"Stop"* (hand out) and *"Think"* (pointing to your brain). Explain that using the word "H.O.W" is a quick way to remember three different strategies! The big, fancy word for that is an "acronym" which means that each letter in that word stands for something. As you explain what each letter stands for, pantomime that action and have the students model the action as well. With each step, allow students the opportunity to discuss and make connections to their school, their community and themselves.

Practice

Guided Practice: Make a large box on the board separated into four quadrants. In each quadrant, write a different time or place at school, for example: READING TIME, LUNCH, RECESS and HALLWAY. Have students either choose one (or to make it really fun, throw a felt ball at the board like a target to hit one) and ask them which strategy for communicating they think would fit best for that time or place and why? Do this for a couple of rounds.

Perform

Independent Practice: Give out crayons or markers and paper and have students create their own posters showing the different ways to communicate. Encourage them to label their posters with the letters of "H.O.W" so that they can remember them more easily! Display these posters around the room to help prompt the different strategies of communicating for the rest of the week.

The Empower Program   Lesson Plan 6

Skill Set: Stop-Skills

Grade Range: K-2

Social Skill: Keeping Your Cool

Big Picture Goal: Development of inhibition and self-control skills.

Common Core Standard Link: CCSS.ELA-LITERACY.CCRA.SL.1

Materials: Talking piece (optional), paper, crayons/markers, stack of papers (or other prop)

Objective: Students will be able to perform the skill steps for *Keeping Your Cool* with partners by acting or drawing scenarios individually, using the skill card as a resource.

Hook

Create an experience: Carry a stack of papers from your desk to the front of the room and as you are talking to your students, drop the papers all over the floor. Pantomime a temper tantrum reaction, complete with yelling and huffing and foot stomping. In your anger, as you pick up one of the papers, rip it in half and then proceed to complain about that too. End your act with a final grunt and sit down in front of your class with your head buried in your hands.

Analyze the experience: Stand up and take a bow. Then pass around a ball or "talking piece" and ask students for feedback on your reaction to having dropped your papers. Jot down some of their ideas on the board as some will reflect the skill steps they will be learning. This will be a valuable resource to refer back to.

Teach

Define the skill: *How to calm down when you are upset.*

Identify the Skill Steps:

1. Mad meatball – Staying in my bubble, squeezing my hands

2. Count to 10 – Use my fingers

3. Take a rising breath – Breath in, rise up 1-2-3

    Hold it, 1-2-3

    Let it out slow, 1-2-3

4. Use an "I-statement" to communicate

Use physical gestures to cue each skill step. For the "mad meatball" model cupping and squeezing your hands back and forth like you were making a meatball. Explain to students that this is a positive way to get their anger out that doesn't hurt someone else. Next, model using your fingers to count to ten. For the "rising breath" begin by placing your hand on your chest (you may want to stand sideways to show students your profile). Now take a deep breath in counting 1-2-3 silently with your other hand (showing students how your chest actually rises up). Next hold it for 1-2-3 seconds, and then slowly let the breath out for 1-2-3 seconds. Have students practice with you. Finally, ask students if they remember what "I-statements" were from the social skill "COMMUNICATION"? Model using these statements to communicate what students need, want or feel. With each step, allow students the opportunity to discuss and make connections to their school, their community and themselves.

Practice

Guided Practice: Ask students for a time that they remember feeling really mad. Do a group visualization of that scenario by asking students to close their eyes as you describe where they are and what is happening around them in this scenario. Have students go through each step of the social skill with you. You might want to add some reflective self-talk as you go such as, when making a "mad meatball" with your hands saying something like, "wow I feel so mad, but at least I'm not going to get in more trouble by using my hands to hit my little brother . . . "

Perform

Independent Practice: Offer students the choice to either get into pairs and act out scenes that have happened to them only now adding the social skill steps or draw a side-by-side picture of those scenes by themselves. For the partner choice, have one student act while their partner practices guiding them through using the "Helper Prompts" and checking to make sure they hit each step. Then partners can switch. For the side-by-side drawing, instruct students to fold a piece of paper in half and draw a line down the middle where it was folded. One side will be a picture of them getting mad and not using the social skill. The other side will be a picture of what they might look like when they do use the social skill steps and thus "keep their cool." You can even have students label the pictures with simply boxing the first picture in the color red (indicating a negative choice) and boxing the second picture in the color green (indicating a positive choice). Ask students, "Has there ever been a time when you got mad and could have used this skill?"

The Empower Program   Lesson Plan 7

Skill Set: Stop-Skills

Grade Range: K-2

Social Skill: Time and Place

Big Picture Goal: Development of inhibition and self-control skills

Common Core Standard Link: CCSS.ELA-LITERACY.CCRA.SL.1

Materials: Talking piece (optional), index cards, paper, (options of: fly swatters, flashlights, white boards)

Objective: Students will be able to perform the skill steps of *Time and Place* by engaging in a group game, using the skill card as a resource.

Hook

Create an experience: Using either the board or index cards (or if you really want to be creative, make puzzle large pieces) and place the following words (or pictures) on each: LUNCH, GYM, EAT, RUN AROUND. Ask your students if anyone can make a match without you telling them anything else about the words or pictures? If students do this automatically, compliment them on their quick thinking! If they struggle, model matching RUN AROUND and LUNCH and ask if that makes any sense? Then try EAT and LUNCH and ask if that's better. Continue until you get the following matching pairs: LUNCH-EAT, GYM-RUN AROUND.

Analyze the experience: Pass around a ball or "talking piece" and ask students why it was that they matched each word or picture? Facilitate a conversation about how there seem to be different times and places where certain actions are better than others or make more sense. You can also use this time to re-match the words incorrectly such as "EAT-RUN AROUND" and ask students why that wouldn't make sense or why that might be a problem?

Teach

Define the skill: *How to make good choices in different places.*

Identify the Skill Steps:

1. Stop and think – *"Right now I am at _____, and it's time for _____."*

2. Mind Hop – *"If I _____, _____ might happen . . . "*

3. Make a green choice – *"I can choose to _____!"*

Use physical gestures to cue each skill step such as having students follow the leader as you use your hand to cue *"Stop"* (hand out) and *"Think"* (pointing to your brain). For the next step, have students point to their brain and make two jumps with their finger as they say, *"If I* [insert finger hop #1], *this* [insert finger hop #2] *will happen."* Give an example such as, *"If I throw a temper tantrum, I will get into more trouble"* as you "mind hop" from the cause to the effect. For the last step, cue students to make a "green" or positive choice. Use the self-determining statement *"I can ___"* and have them echo with a better choice than your example. With each step, allow students the opportunity to discuss and make connections to their school, their community and themselves.

Practice

Guided Practice: Draw several circles on the board (or you can use pieces of paper on the floor) with different times (ex. lunch, reading, transition, morning arrival, recess, seatwork, etc.) and different places (ex. classroom, hallway, bathroom, gymnasium, outside, etc.). Explain to students that you will now be playing a relay race game using fly swatters on the board (or another rendition that works better for your space such as flashlights shining on the right answer or white boards where the students race to write the correct answer instead). Choose two students who are showing excellent social skills (you can even cue that you are calling on them due to a *known social skill* such as body position!) Line the two students up side by side a decent distance from the board standing next to each other. Tell the students that you will be giving them an example of an action and their goal is to run up to the board and try and "swat" (or shine the light or write on their whiteboard) what time or place would be the best match for that action. You might, for instance say, "Eating a sandwich" to which you would want students to swat the circle with the word or picture for "Lunch" or "Cafeteria." This may also result in a tie where one child chooses a correct time and the other finds the place. This is a great chance to discuss that sometimes both can be true and then pull for when, in the same place, might NOT be the right time to "eat lunch" (such as during an assembly or as you are walking to the bathroom).

Perform

Play this game as a whole group, calling students up who are demonstrating excellent social skills!

The Empower Program   **Lesson Plan 8**
Skill Set: Stop-Skills
Grade Range: K-2

Social Skill: Waiting

Big Picture Goal: Development of inhibition and self-control skills

Common Core Standard Link: CCSS.ELA-LITERACY.CCRA.SL.1

Materials: Talking piece (optional), dice/spinner or deck of cards

Objective: Students will be able to perform the skill steps for *Waiting* in a small group using the skill card as a resource.

Hook

Create an experience: Tell your students a story about a time when you personally had to wait for something. Be very dramatic and feel free to act out your many tantrum moments, especially by using your hands to fiddle with things while you were waiting and perhaps even getting into trouble *because* of your fiddling or impatience. You can also use the following story as a guide:

"When I was little I loved mint chocolate chip ice cream! I loved it so much that when my mom brought some home, I would get so excited to eat it that I would eat all my vegetables, do all my homework and then stand by the refrigerator waiting for ice cream time to come! One day though, my cousins were over to visit. I had eight cousins and they were all guests in our house. This meant that I had to wait even longer for my beloved mint chocolate chip ice cream moment to come! My mom had us all sit at the table and wait. She scooped some for my smallest cousin first, then the next one, then the next. As each of my cousins got their ice cream and started to eat it I got more and more mad that I didn't have mine yet! What if they eat ALL the ice cream and there's none left for me? As I watched them eat, I started to get a little more mad and began to bang my hands on the table. My mother came in and told me to stop and that I was being rude. I was even MORE mad now, so I waited until my mother went back into the kitchen and then grabbed my cousins ice cream and plunged the spoon in all the way down to get a big bite. But just as I was about to put that sweet, delicious ice cream in my mouth, my mother came back and took the cup away and told me to go to my room. Now I can't have ice cream for a whole week! It was the worst day!"

Analyze the experience: Pass around a ball or "talking piece" and ask students to give you some advice about what you should have done differently. If students simply say *"I think you should have just waited"* take that opportunity to explain to them just how hard it is for you to just sit there and wait! Ask them to give you specific ways. You can then tell them that thankfully, you learned a cool trick to help you and that is what you are going to teach them next!

Teach

Define the skill: *How you let someone know what you need, want or feel.*

Identify the Skill Steps:

1. Stop and check – Am I in my bubble?
2. Match, Shrink and Squash the time as you wait! (use physical gestures below)

(Hand Motions)

MATCH: slowly touch both thumbs, then each finger together (matching)

SHRINK: while still touching fingertips together, bring them all together (shrinking)

SQUASH: interlace your fingers together (squashing)

Use physical gestures to cue *"Stop"* (hand out) and *"Check"* (using your hands to form a bubble for your personal space measure). The second step includes three hand motions which allow students to do something with their hands that is not going to get them in trouble, while distracting them from the arduous task of just standing around waiting. First, have students use their hands to *"Match"* by slowly touching both of their thumbs, then each finger together, like an evil genius would. Second, have students use their hands to *"Shrink"* the time by bringing all of their fingers tips together without letting any opposite fingers come apart (as if your shrinking something down to a tiny size). Finally, have students *"Squash"* the time by quickly interlacing their fingers so they are now folded. With each step, allow students the opportunity to discuss and make connections to their school, their community and themselves.

Practice

Modeling the activity: Take out a die (or number spinner or deck of cards) and call a student up to roll (or spin or choose a card). Whatever number they land on, challenge them to wait, shrink and squash the time that many rounds while they freeze and stay in their bubble. For example, if the student rolled a 4, they would go through the hand motions, as a series of three, 4 times. Once they have completed their rounds praise them and give them that many "waiting points" for the game.

Perform

Independent Practice: Now separate your students into pairs or groups of 3 or more (your choice) and pass out either a die to each group (or a spinner or small stack of cards with numbers on them) and give them each an index card to keep track of their points. The object of the game is to see who can wait the longest (while doing their rounds of hand motions completely for each turn). This may sound too good to be true, but with a game-like spin to it and adding points, this is an excellent and engaging way to have them practice their new strategy of physically coping with the concept of patience!

The Empower Program   **Lesson Plan 9**

Skill Set: Stop-Skills

Grade Range: K-2

Social Skill: Asking For Attention

Big Picture Goal: Development of inhibition and self-control skills.

Common Core Standard Link: CCSS.ELA-LITERACY.CCRA.SL.1

Materials: Talking piece (optional),

Objective: Students will be able to perform the skill steps for *Asking For Attention* in teams by creating a skit and using the skill cards as a resource.

Hook

Create an experience: Ask students for a volunteer who would like to do a skit with you and play the role of the teacher. Remind them that you will be choosing someone who has been showing you excellent "T.F.B" (Tone, Face and Body Position). When the student comes up, tell them that you would like them to teach the class the ABC's and then take their seat and assume the role of student. As the, now teacher, student begins teaching, yell out "I need to go to the bathroom!" then walk up and begin poking the "teacher" and asking over and over. You can even go back to your seat and then begin to whine with your hand raised as you do so. Give the student teacher a round of applause and then end the skit.

Analyze the experience: Pass a ball or "talking piece" around and ask students what they thought of how you asked for the teachers' attention? Defend the fact that you did technically *ask*, and challenge students to be specific as to why your way of asking was not working or was causing a problem. If they say it wasn't a good choice, ask them for reasons why. Ask the "student teachers" how *they* felt when you chose to poke them and whine? Then proceed to transition to teaching the skill steps as validation of their feelings and reasons.

Teach

Define the skill: *How to ask when you need attention.*

Identify the Skill Steps:

1. Stop and think – What is the <u>TIME</u> and <u>PLACE</u> right now?

2. Ask yourself H.O.W – "H.O.W can I ask for attention?"

> **H** – Raise my <u>hand</u> or use a signal
>
> **O** – Write or draw it <u>on paper</u>
>
> **W** – I can use my <u>words</u>

Use physical gestures to cue *"Stop"* (hand out) and *"Think"* (pointing to your brain). Remind students of the social skill they already learned (Time and Place) as you model asking yourself, *"What is the time and place right now?"* Give an example such as, *"Right now it's the morning and we are at school."* For the second step, pantomime a light bulb going off in your brain and ask students if anyone remembers what the letters in H.O.W stand for from our social skill of "Communication"? Remind students that it stands for <u>H</u>and, <u>O</u>n paper, and using <u>W</u>ords to communicate. With each step, allow students the opportunity to discuss and make connections to their school, their community and themselves.

Practice

Guided Practice: Write "H.O.W" on the board and explain that you will be splitting the class into three teams: the H-team, the O-team and the W-team. Each team will work together (or in pairs if necessary) to make up their own skits showing how to use each letter of the strategy to ask for attention in a positive way at school. Model this using the same student you chose for your ABC's lesson only this time, say you will pretend you are on the H-team and show how to appropriately raise your hand while you wait to be called on. You may also want to model how to use multiple students in the skit for different roles so that larger groups have an idea of how to create a skit with more than two roles. Give the teams an allotted amount of time to create their skits and you facilitate by walking around and giving feedback.

Perform

Independent Practice: Call each team up (or a pair from each team) to perform their skit for the class.

The Empower Program   **Lesson Plan 10**

Skill Set: Stop-Skills

Grade Range: K-2

Social Skill: Listening Position

Big Picture Goal: Development of inhibition and self-control skills.

Common Core Standard Link: CCSS.ELA-LITERACY.CCRA.SL.1

Materials: Talking piece (optional), paper, crayons

Objective: Students will be able to perform the skill steps for *Listening Position* by drawing individually or acting them out in groups using the skill card as a resource.

Hook

Create an experience: Gather students to play a game of telephone by having everyone sit in a circle. Explain that in this game, *"the first person in the circle will have a special message written on a piece of paper and will whisper it in the ear of the person sitting next to them."* (If students are too young to read, have another adult whisper the message to them to start). *"Then we will continue to whisper the message to each other around the circle until it reaches the end."* Create instant excitement by then informing your students that, *"If the message travels all the way around the circle successfully and the last person says what's written on the secret paper, everyone will get an ice cream sundae!"* (or some other ridiculous reward that seems too good to be true and will engage serious effort). Now position yourself NOT as the first person to read and deliver the message, but instead as the 3rd or 4th recipient. On the first go-round, stare out the window as the student sitting next to you is whispering the message to you. Look distracted and clearly not paying attention. When the group becomes agitated that you are ruining their chances for the reward, tell them that you are going to start over. Next time through, when it gets to your turn, as the person begins to talk, start talking to them about what you had for breakfast this morning or something else unrelated. When the group complains, again apologize and say you'll try it one more time. This time as your turn approaches, simply stand up and walk away from the circle and go to your desk to do something. Come back to the group and say, "oh forget it, everyone back to their seats" and await the groans.

Analyze the experience: Pass around a ball or "talking piece" and ask students why they felt the game didn't go well? If students mention anything about your body position, your unrelated talking or your eyes not being on your partner note this on the board or draw a quick picture of it. You can refer to their ideas next when introducing each step of the social skill to increase buy-in and support for the steps!

Teach

Define the skill: *How to show someone you are ready and listening.*

Identify the Skill Steps:

1. Head up
2. Voice off
3. Body calm
4. Eyes on

Use physical gestures to cue all of these skill steps! Start with your hand under your chin to cue head up, finger over your lips for voice off, hands by your sides (or making a column down your sides from top to bottom) for body calm, and fingers pointing from your eyes forward for eyes on. Once your students are familiar with each gesture, you can begin to go through the gestures faster and faster to make this more engaging (like the song "Head, shoulders, knees and toes")!

Practice

Guided Practice: You can give students a choice of how they would like to practice here. They can either choose to create a "LP" or "Listening Position" poster that illustrates all four steps of the skill, or they can work with a partner to see how fast they can show and say all four steps as a team. For the team activity, model with a student partner by designating one of you as the "voice" and the other as the "actions." Now, if you are the voice, stand behind (or kneel) your partner and have them do the hand gestures of each step as they silently mouth the words that you are verbally saying.

Perform

Independent Practice: Have students choose their practice activity (drawing a poster individually or working as a team to act out the steps as fast as they can) and begin working.

The Empower Program   Lesson Plan 11

Skill Set: Simmer-Skills

Grade Range: K-2

Social Skill: Handling Frustration

Big Picture Goal: Development of emotional self-regulation skills.

Common Core Standard Link: CCSS.ELA-LITERACY.CCRA.SL.1

Materials: Talking piece (optional), toy, paper, string, scissors, (optional: pre-cut hand shapes)

Objective: Students will be able to perform the skill steps for *Handling Frustration* by creating a tool belt of hands showing each strategy, using the skill card as a resource.

Hook

Create an experience: Choose a toy or other tangible object that you can assemble in some way. Gather students for the lesson and say "just hold on one second while I put this back together to put it away . . . " Then proceed to become visibly frustrated by the process of (for instance with a set of Jenga blocks) of trying to put the blocks back into the box, having problems, getting angry, shoving them, trying to shove them harder and then becoming so frustrated that you slam them all over the floor. Exhale and throw your hands up in the air!

Analyze the experience: Pass around a ball or "talking piece" and have students give you feedback on what they just saw you do. Facilitate comments about your frustration and if a student says the word frustration, praise them for their vocabulary and write it on the board. If not, engage a discussion about how you were feeling and pull for feeling words. Use this as an opportunity to talk about the word frustrated and what being frustrated means.

Teach

Define the skill: *How to let out frustration in a positive way.*

Identify the Skill Steps:

1. Stop and think – Plan in my hand!

2. <u>HAND</u>ling this up or down?

       Up – Hand up to talk it out

       Up – Hand up to ask for space

       Down – Hand down to draw or write it out

       Down – Hand down to make a mad meatball

Use physical gestures to cue *"Stop"* (hand out) and *"Think"* (pointing to your brain). Prompt that students already have a "plan in their hand" by using your hand to pantomime each of four choices they have to use their hand to appropriately ask for what they need to handle their frustration. Hold your hand up to indicate one of two choices where students can raise their hand to either ask to talk out their frustration or ask for time and space to calm down if they aren't ready to talk about it yet. Hold your hand down next and pantomime using your hand to write or draw out your frustration on a piece of paper or to squeeze your hands together to make a "mad meatball" instead of using them to get you in trouble.

Practice

Guided Practice: Explain to students that they will be making a "tool belt" today as a fun way of showing all the tools they have right in their own hands to "<u>HAND</u>le" their frustration using the social skill steps they just learned. Model tracing your hand on a piece of paper or having a student help you do so. Then stack 3 more sheets of paper behind it and cut out your hand outline revealing 4 blank hands. **If you have very young students, having pre-cut out hands may be easier! Use each hand to write or draw each strategy (raise hand to talk, raise hand to ask for time/space, use hand to write, use hands to squeeze together). Now take some string (or whatever you have handy) and either tape or clip the hands to the string and tie it around your waist! Tell students that you are going to use your handy tool belt to help you <u>HAND</u>le your frustration for the rest of the day!

Perform

Independent Practice: Give out materials and facilitate with students completing the hands-on activity

The Empower Program   Lesson Plan 12

Skill Set: Simmer-Skills

Grade Range: K-2

Social Skill: Communicating Frustration

Big Picture Goal: Development of emotional self-regulation skills.

Common Core Standard Link: CCSS.ELA-LITERACY.CCRA.SL.1

Materials: Talking piece (optional), balloon, paper, crayons

1. **Objective:** Students will be able to perform skill steps for *Communicating Frustration* by sharing their quadrant boxes with I-statements and using the skill card as a resource.

Hook

Create an experience: Get your balloon (and your nerves) ready. Pass out post-it notes or do this verbally for younger students and ask, "What is a time when you were really frustrated?" If the meaning of the word frustrated is confusing, use this as an opportunity to define it and give examples. Each time a student shares an idea, act frustrated with them as you agree and blow a small amount of air into the balloon. As you go around, for each idea blow more air into the balloon until it POPS!

Analyze the experience: Pass a ball or "talking piece" around and ask students why the balloon popped? Use the idea of "too much air in there" or something along that line to act as a physical metaphor for what happens sometimes when we keep our frustration in instead of communicating it. Now choose an interpersonal example and ask students how they think they should communicate that frustration to the other person. Before they answer, jump in and say, "I have it, what about hitting them? That would let them know that they made me mad right?" Wait for students to discourage you and ask, "Why isn't that a good idea?" Then say, "Well what about calling them a name back?" etc. Give several non-examples and then ask students if they have any ideas about what a more positive way would be to communicate their frustration? Now use some of their ideas to transition to teaching them the skill steps so they don't POP like the balloon!

Teach

Define the skill: *How to tell someone you are frustrated.*

Identify the Skill Steps:

1. Stop and breath
2. Use a calm tone
3. Say, *"Excuse me"*
4. Use an "I-statement"

      "I didn't like it when _____"

      "I feel _____"

      "I need you to _____"

Use physical gestures to cue *"Stop"* (hand out) and *"Breath"* (modeling a deep breath). Explain that a deep breath helps us give oxygen to our brain and we need our brains to think of making positive choices! If we think when we are mad, we are probably going to make mad choices. For the second step, ask if students can show a calm tone as they say the words "calm tone." For the third step, explain that saying, "Excuse me" shows that you are in control of your anger, even though you can still be angry. You can also add that it shows adults like teachers that you are thinking about making a good social skills choice, even though you are frustrated! Finally, model using the "I-statements" listed in the skill steps, as well as adding in any of your own.

Practice

Guided Practice: Take a piece of paper and fold it in half then in half again. Unfold the paper to reveal four boxes. In each box write one of the I-statements given in the social skill. Leave the forth box blank. You can prepare these in advance for younger students or use this as a writing activity for older students. Now explain to students that you are going to draw a picture of four different times when you are frustrated and can use the I-statements in each box. The last box is a free choice box where you want to see their creativity and see what kind of I-statement they can come up with!

Perform

Independent Practice: Pass out papers and crayons and allow students to begin working on their quadrant pictures. Walk around facilitating this process actively and verbally point out great work to keep them motivated! Students share when completed.

The Empower Program   **Lesson Plan 13**

Skill Set: Simmer-Skills

Grade Range: K-2

Social Skill: Moving On

Big Picture Goal: Development of emotional self-regulation skills.

Common Core Standard Link: CCSS.ELA-LITERACY.CCRA.SL.1

Materials: Talking piece (optional), rope, signs saying "NO CARTOONS", paper

Objective: Students will be able to perform skill steps for *Moving On* after drawing past and present examples and share skill steps using the skill card as a resource.

Hook

Create an experience: Get a rope of some sort and put a sign on it that says "NO CARTOONS" and tie one end to a door or something steady. Invite two students to come up to the front of the class and explain that they will be playing siblings at home. Explain to the class that these two siblings just had a fight over [insert timely toy or game] and were told that they couldn't watch cartoons for the rest of the night. Tell one student to look mad and maybe even throw a 5-second temper tantrum and the other student to look mad as well. As the pretend parent, tell the two siblings that they need to go and start their homework. Now whisper to the student who was throwing the tantrum to hold the other end of the rope that says "NO CARTOONS" and keep complaining about what had happened. Whisper to the second student to pretend to go to their desk and start their pretend homework. As this happens, thank the second student for moving on while you go to the first student and say, "You know _____ if you keep this up, you are going to lose your cartoon time for tomorrow as well as today . . . " (Coax the student to keep complaining). Go back over to the student pretending to do their homework and praise them as you tell them to go wash up and get ready for dinner. Go back to the first student and say, "well now you haven't even started your homework, and you have lost your cartoon time for tomorrow . . . " Stop the skit and tell each student to take a bow.

Analyze the experience: Pass a ball or "talking piece" around and have students offer feedback about the skit. Ask questions about what they thought of the choices that each sibling made? Then take the "NO CARTOONS" sign and flip it over and write "PAST" on it. Explain that you are going to teach a social skill about how to move on from things that happened in the past so you can enjoy more positive things like the second student did, instead of getting caught up in being mad and only getting into more trouble like the first student.

Teach

Define the skill: *How to move past a mistake.*

Identify the Skill Steps:

1. Take a rising breath

2. Think *"Blast the past, open the present!"*

3. Imagine your present

Ask students if they remember how to take a rising breath? Model the three steps (breath in rising up 1-2-3, hold it 1-2-3, let it out slow 1-2-3). For the second step, pantomime burying the thing that you are super mad about into the ground. Tell the students what's in the past is done, and while we can't do anything about it, sometimes it still makes us really mad! So, since we can't change it, let's blow it up so we can move on (and get some of our aggression out too!). Pantomime, pushing down a lever and making a blow up sound (or a button detonator or whatever other imaginative, cathartic maneuver you wish). Now, brush off your brow and say, "Well that's over. Blast the past!" Now tell students that what's left over is "the present" and explain to them that the present can mean two things. Draw a box with a bow on it (or show a picture of a gift) and ask students what this kind of present is? Then point to your feet and the clock and say, "another kind of present is the NOW, the time and place we are right here and right now!" This is the kind of present you get when you move on and decide to make a positive choice, even if you weren't happy about something that happened in the past. This kind of present is very special because if you move on, you might find that you will get more positive things to come your way than if you stayed in the past and kept being angry about what happened then.

Practice

Guided Practice: Draw a T-chart on the board and write "Stay in the PAST" on one side and "Open the PRESENT" on the other side. Brainstorm negative things that could happen if they stay in the past, as well as positive things that could happen if they move on to the present?

Perform

Independent Practice: Have students fold a piece of paper in half to create two sections. Tell students to label the first half "Stay in the PAST" and the other half "Open the PRESENT." Now have them choose any of the ideas on the board or they can come up with their own personal examples, and draw a picture of each under the label. Students share out when done.

The Empower Program   Lesson Plan 14

Skill Set: Simmer-Skills

Grade Range: K-2

Social Skill: Accepting Consequences

Big Picture Goal: Development of emotional self-regulation skills.

Common Core Standard Link: CCSS.ELA-LITERACY.CCRA.SL.1

Materials: Talking piece (optional), cup of milk/water, cookies, paper towels

Objective: Students will be able to create a post card of skill steps for *Accepting Consequences*, using skill card as a resource, for future independent use.

Hook

Create an experience: Bring in a cup of milk (or water) and some cookies. Place these materials on a table visible to all students (away from anything electronic!). Place a role of paper towels on the same table. Now begin to start your lesson saying that you are so excited to enjoy your milk and cookies and bump into the table, knocking over the milk. Look down at the spilling milk and instead of starting to clean it up, say, "I didn't do it, it's not my fault . . . this is horrible . . . umm . . . umm" but all the while just staring at the spilled milk. Frantically ask your students what you should do!

Analyze the experience: Pass a ball or "talking piece" around and discuss what just happened. Tell students that you were so upset about what happened that you didn't even want to admit you did it, even though it was an accident . . . so you just thought if you said you didn't do it, that would make it all better! Prompt students to give you feedback on how easy it would have been to just grab the paper towels and clean it up, then maybe ask for a new glass of milk. Now explain that the "spilled milk" was a "consequence" which is a fancy word for what happens as a result of something else happening. Give a couple more examples of simple cause-effect relationships that are neutral such as: helping a friend-then smiling, turning the lights off-it being dark, etc. Now explain that you are going to learn a skill that will help you to accept the not-so-fun consequences so that you can move on and enjoy the positive things in life (like cookies!).

Teach

Define the skill: *How to calm down and handle a consequence.*

Identify the Skill Steps:

1. Stop and squeeze – Make a mad meatball

2. Mind Hop – *"If I stay mad, _____ might happen."*

      "If I move on, _____ might happen."

3. Make a green choice!

Use physical gestures to cue each skill step such as having students follow the leader as you use your hand to cue *"Stop"* (hand out) and *"Squeeze"* (making a "mad meatball" with your hands). Tell them to imagine their anger is in between their hands and tell them to squeeze it and mush it into a tiny little ball so it doesn't take over their attitude! For the second step, review how to "mind hop" by putting your hand on your head and saying out loud, "If I stay mad [insert hop motion with finger forward], what will happen?" Ask students to close their eyes and imagine with you what might happen if you stayed mad at the spilled milk and done nothing about it? Then make a rewinding sound (or get your students to help do this) and mind hop again saying, "If I move on, what will happen?" Finally look proud and have students repeat, "I can make a green, or positive choice!"

Practice

Guided Practice: Have students sit in a circle or on the rug and volunteer to call out some negative consequences that they have experienced in the past. Make a list on the board or verbally stop and discuss each one. For each consequence, pantomime throwing your hands up and crying, "over spilled milk" and have the students to do the same. Then put your hands over your eyes and say, "this is horrible!" and have the students do the same. Then peek one eye out of your hands and say, "did anything change?" Since the answer is clearly no (accept maybe getting into trouble for throwing a fit) ask students what they would recommend instead? How could I accept this consequence and move on? Have them act it out or discuss it. Give each praise or have the whole group give a thumbs up.

Perform

Independent Practice: Have students go back to their seats and write themselves a post card reminding them of the steps of the skill "Accepting Consequences" for the next time they end up becoming upset. Save their cards in a safe place and use them when needed, or tape them to their desks for that week.

The Empower Program Lesson Plan 15

Skill Set: Simmer-Skills

Grade Range: K-2

Social Skill: Respectfully Disagreeing

Big Picture Goal: Development of emotional self-regulation skills.

Common Core Standard Link: CCSS.ELA-LITERACY.CCRA.SL.1

Materials: Talking piece (optional), jump rope, paper

Objective: Students will be able to create a drawing showing the skill steps of *Respectfully Disagreeing*, using the skill card as a resource.

Hook

Create an experience: Ask students if they have ever had a disagreement? Then take out a jump rope or rope of some kind and have two volunteers come up and argue over something trivial. Each time the person argues back, have them tug the rope.

Analyze the experience: Pass a ball or "talking piece" around and ask the class what that looked like? Ask them if either student looked like they were getting anywhere with their point? Now invite a student to come up and replace one of the original volunteers. Just before they hold the rope, whisper in their ear that when the other student argues, they are to just say, *"I respectfully disagree"* and drop the rope and walk away. Have the students act this out. Now pass the ball around again and ask how that was different and who looked like they had more control?

Teach

Define the skill: *How to disagree in a respectful way.*

Identify the Skill Steps:

1. Check your T.F.B (Tone, Face and Body)

2. Listen first…

3. If you disagree, use a calm tone and say, *"I respectfully disagree."*

For the first step, remind students to always check their T.F.B (tone of voice, facial expression and body position) to make sure they are not communicating something they don't want to. Giving a "non-example" is also fun and helpful for illustrating this. For the next step, tell students that listening is a powerful tool! People that listen and show control get more information than those who just start talking themselves. Finally, model how to listen first and then reply, "I respectfully disagree." Explain to students that you always have the right to disagree, though that may not change what happens. Give examples.

Practice

Guided Practice: Have students volunteer situations where they have argued with someone about something and gone back and forth like a tug-of-war? Write these on the board. Now have students come up and act out one or two scenarios using the social skill and not using the social skill. Again, reiterate how much more in control the social skills version looks as opposed to the arguing version. Explain that "confident kids" don't need to argue and yell and scream. You can prompt this throughout the day and compliment students who are showing this "confidence" by using the social skill.

Perform

Independent Practice: Have students create their own picture of themselves showing that they are "confident kids" by respectfully disagreeing and "dropping the rope" as shown earlier in the lesson. They can either draw one picture showing this or fold their paper in half and show the social skills way and also the non-social skills way.

The Empower Program   **Lesson Plan 16**

Skill Set: Solve-Skills

Grade Range: K-2

Social Skill: Communicating Concerns

Big Picture Goal: Development of problem solving skills.

Common Core Standard Link: CCSS.ELA-LITERACY.CCRA.SL.1

Materials: Talking piece (optional)

Objective: Students will be able to perform, in a small group, the skill steps for *Communicating Concerns*, given scenarios and using the skill card as a resource.

Hook

Create an experience: Gather the class for a discussion and while you have everyone's attention, have another adult (or set up a student) to bump into you by accident. Loudly react by screaming, "hey watch where you're going!" and give a nasty look.

Analyze the experience: Pass a ball or "talking piece" around and ask students to give you feedback on how that looked and also, how they think the other person felt? Explain that today, you will be teaching a social skill that allows you to communicate to someone else that you have a problem, without turning it into a larger problem or coming off as the problem yourself.

Teach

Define the skill: *How to tell someone when you have a problem in a respectful way.*

Identify the Skill Steps:

1. Check your T.F.B (Tone-Face-Body)

2. Say, *"Excuse me, I have a concern"*

3. Use an "I-statement"

   "I didn't like it when you _____."

4. Listen as they respond

Begin by writing the word concern on the board and ask students to brainstorm (using a web if needed) what do they think that word means? For the first step, call on a student and ask if they remember what three social skills "T.F.B" stands for? Once you have discussed that they stand for Tone of Voice, Facial Expression and Body Position, call on another student to ask what checking your T.F.B might mean? For the second step, explain that when you are communicating a concern, it is important to remain in control and use the words *"Excuse me"* to show that you are in control and *"Concern"* is a very respectful way of saying you have a problem. Remind students how to use "I-statements" and brainstorm several different types of I-statements for different scenarios. Finally, stress that the last step of listening as the other person responds is very important! If we don't listen to the other person, how can we expect them to listen to us when we communicate our concerns in the future?

Practice

Guided Practice: Write several bubbles on the board and brainstorm key words for each bubble that note scenarios that could spark concerns. Now invite two students to come to the front of the room to model how to use the social skill steps to communicate that concern. Make sure that you also coach the other student to ask, *"What's your concern?"* after the first student says they have one. This step is not in the skill steps because kids can't always count on someone else being as respectful, however in your classroom community, urge students to make sure they show respect by responding this way. Make sure that they know that just because they say, *"what's your concern?"* doesn't mean that they are guilty of anything. It just shows that they are listening and showing respect.

Perform

Independent Practice: Have students form groups of two or more and practice the rest of the remaining scenarios from the bubbles independently. Move around the room coaching and praising their use of skills they already learned (such as tone, face, body and listening position).

The Empower Program   Lesson Plan 17

Skill Set: Solve-Skills

Grade Range: K-2

Social Skill: Joining A Group

Big Picture Goal: Development of problem solving skills.

Common Core Standard Link: CCSS.ELA-LITERACY.CCRA.SL.1

Materials: Talking piece (optional),

Objective: Students will be able to perform a skit showing the skill steps for *Joining A Group* and using the skill card as a resource.

Hook

Create an experience: Ask students to raise their hand if they have younger brothers, sisters or cousins. Ask them to now raise their eyebrows if they have ever had a problem with those younger kids barging into their games or trying to join their friends when you didn't want them to. Now, tell students a story about a time when you were younger and playing with your friends and this happened to you. Use the story below or make up your own:

When I was younger I loved building really tall towers with my set of blocks. My two friends would come over and we would have contests to see how tall we could build our tower before it fell over. We would all stand around the tower in a circle to protect it and it was so much fun! The problem was that I had a younger brother growing up and he was only 4 years old. One day, he came running into the room shouting, "I want to play, I want to play!" and before we could tell him what we were doing, he knocked everything over. We were so mad that we yelled at him and told him to leave us alone. Then we ALL got in trouble because my Mom said that we were being mean to my brother and we HAD to let him join us. All we were trying to do was tell her that we wanted him to listen to our rules of the game before just barging in. What a mess.

Analyze the experience: Pass a ball or "talking piece" around and ask students for comments, feedback and connections. Explain that today, they will be learning a social skill that they can use to help them if they want to join groups, but that they can also teach their younger siblings and cousins and become a social skills leader themselves!

Teach

Define the skill: *How to ask to become part of a group.*

Identify the Skill Steps:

1. Use a calm tone of voice

2. Say, *"Excuse me, may I join you?"*

3. Listen for the group to answer . . .

4. Say, *"Thank you"* if they say yes

    Say, *"Ok"* if they say no and move on to another choice

For the first step, ask students what social skill they think would help if they need to ask a question? There are several correct answers here, but this will help to remind them of how many social skills they have already learned! Cue that using a calm tone of voice will help them to not only be heard by the group, but also sound like someone that a group would want to include! For the second step, remind them that using the term *"Excuse me"* does two things – first, it sets a tone of respect and second, it lets the group know you need their attention. For the third step, coach students to remember to wait and listen before just joining in. Sometimes a group may not be ready to include another person and waiting for their response shows that you understand that. Connect back to your story about your little brother and how he knocked all the blocks over and made you mad because he didn't wait for you to tell him what you were playing. Finally, explain that if the group says yes, remember to thank them! If the group says no for whatever reason, coach students to say "ok" and make another choice. Explain that the choice could involve politely asking why they cannot join and having a conversation about it, but it could also mean just choosing another activity and moving on.

Practice

Guided Practice: Ask a few students to volunteer to come up and model an example skit of what this skill would look like in a classroom example. Have the class coach the group in choosing an example and all pitch in to remind each student of the steps.

Perform

Independent Practice: Break the class into small groups and give them an allotted amount of time to come up with their own skit showing the skill steps. Invite them to use scenarios from school, after school, home or anywhere else they would like. When time is up, have groups perform their skits for the class.

The Empower Program   **Lesson Plan 18**

Skill Set: Solve-Skills

Grade Range: K-2

Social Skill: Compromise

Big Picture Goal: Development of problem solving skills.

Common Core Standard Link: CCSS.ELA-LITERACY.CCRA.SL.1

Materials: Talking piece (optional), (choice: toy or food), timer, paper, crayons

Objective: Students will be able to perform a skit showing the skill steps for *Compromise* in a small group using a given scenario and the skill card as a resource.

Hook

Create an experience: Show students a cool new toy or a delicious looking food item (such as a cupcake or cookie). Ask for two volunteers. Place the toy on the table (so everyone can see) and tell the two students that they have to find a solution where they can BOTH enjoy the toy or food item and AGREE on it in order to use it. Tell them that they have 2 minutes to figure out how and they can use the rest of the class to help if they want. Set a timer and begin.

Analyze the experience: Regardless of how the experiment went (good or bad), have the students go back to their seats and pass a ball or "talking piece" around to analyze the experiment. Ask students what they thought the two students did well and where they might have been able to use other ideas. Now explain that today, you will be teaching them a social skill that helps in situations where both people want something and need to figure out a solution.

Teach

Define the skill: *How to find a solution that both people agree on.*

Identify the Skill Steps:

1. Stop and think – How can we both get what we want?

2. Listen to what they want

3. Say what you want

4. Talk about how you can agree or try:

    - Taking turns using a timer

    - Sharing or working together

    - Asking for help together

You can start by drawing the following diagram on the board: YOU → BOTH ← ME. Ask students what the word "both" means? Ask for examples where not just you, or just me, but both of us have to work together to do something that we both want? One example of this is a seesaw on the playground. It's pretty boring to try and ride on a seesaw by yourself, but when both kids work together, it can be really fun! Clarify this first step by saying that not all things are like a seesaw and sometimes it can take a little brainwork to figure out how to both get what we want. For the second step, point to your ear and say *"Listen to what they want . . . "* Explain that having good social skills means showing listening, even if you want the same thing. Then prompt to say what you want. Finally, talk about how you can agree. You can ask students for their ideas here or offer the three ideas above.

Practice

Guided Practice: Have students brainstorm things that they usually have issues sharing or "compromising" with during the school day or at home. Write these ideas on the board. Now ask for a group of two or more students to volunteer to come up and act out one of the scenarios using the skill steps they just learned.

Perform

Independent Practice: Have students work in small groups to create skits about one of the other scenarios on the board or have them journal or draw a picture of themselves using the skill steps for their own scenario either in school or at home.

The Empower Program   Lesson Plan 19

Skill Set: Solve-Skills

Grade Range: K-2

Social Skill: Problem Solving

Big Picture Goal: Development of problem solving skills.

Common Core Standard Link: CCSS.ELA-LITERACY.CCRA.SL.1

Materials: Talking piece (optional), blocks (or anything else you can "clean up"), cardboard box, paper, crayons

Objective: Students will be able to illustrate the skill steps for *Problem Solving* on individual posters using their own scenarios and the skill cards as a resource.

Hook

Create an experience: Gather students around and explain that before you start the lesson, you just need to clean up all of these blocks (or any other objects you have handy) that are all over the floor. Pick up a cardboard box (without securing the bottom) and begin putting the items into the box. As they fall out of the bottom, become frustrated and try again to put them back in. Finally throw the box on the floor and yell out, *"This isn't working! I give up!"*

Analyze the experience: Tell students that the social skill that they will be learning today is called "Problem Solving" so maybe you should just go on and introduce the skill steps and maybe *they* can help you use them to solve *your* problem with the box.

Teach

Define the skill: *How to make a problem better.*

Identify the Skill Steps:

1. Take a rising breath

2. Make a picture of the problem

3. Circle the part that you want to fix

4. Pick a fix:

    - Use a social skill to fix it yourself

    - Ask for help from someone else

Ask if students can review what a rising breath is and how to do it? (Since you could use the help being frustrated from the box fiasco!) Remind them that it has three parts: hand on their chest and inhale up 1-2-3 seconds, hold it there (chest risen) 1-2-3 seconds, and out slow 1-2-3 seconds. For the next step, explain that sometimes problems can be much easier to solve when you can see them, like a picture. Explain that, even adults sometimes draw pictures of problems so they can solve them better such as architects, engineers and scientists to name a few. Now demonstrate this by drawing a picture of the box on the board. For the third step, call on a volunteer to come up to the board and circle the part of the problem we want to fix? After having them circle or draw an arrow to the bottom of the box, explain that now we need to pick a way to fix it. Have students point to their brains and repeat after you, *"Use an idea or social skill to fix it yourself."* Ask if any students have any ideas or social skills that might help to fix the problem? Finally, if that doesn't work, ask students to repeat as you say, *"Ask for help from someone else."*

Practice

Guided Practice: Explain that the box problem was an easy one to fix, but social problems can seem much harder! Ask students to raise their hands and suggest problems that they have had with friends, classmates or siblings. Now choose one and have a couple of volunteers come to the front of the room to act out each step of the skill as the class guides them through connecting the steps to that social problem.

Perform

Independent Practice: Give out paper and crayons and ask students to fold their paper in half and then half again (revealing 4 quadrants when unfolded). Have students label each box 1-4. Then have them illustrate the steps to this skill with their own scenario (a social or physical problem) and show each step using their poster.

The Empower Program   Lesson Plan 20

Skill Set: Solve-Skills

Grade Range: K-2

Social Skill: Choosing Who Goes First

Big Picture Goal: Development of problem solving skills.

Common Core Standard Link: CCSS.ELA-LITERACY.CCRA.SL.1

Materials: Talking piece (optional), coin, paper, crayons

Objective: Students will be able to create a poster and teach another student the skill steps for *Choosing Who Goes First*, individually or in small groups, using the skill card as a resource.

Hook

Create an experience: Ask students if they have ever gotten into a fight trying to figure out who went first playing a game? Ask for stories and allow the students to have fun telling them (home, school, any context). Remind students that if the story includes other people, to leave their names out so we don't hurt anyone's feelings.

Analyze the experience: Ask students for feedback on what all of the stories had in common? Highlight ideas that uncover the fighting over who went first often delayed the game playing further than simply choosing or even caused the game not to be played at all, or worse, people to get into trouble or not want to play with each other at all.

Teach

Define the skill: *How to choose who goes first in a fair way.*

Identify the Skill Steps:

Pick a strategy

1. Rock-Paper-Scissor

    - Play Rock-Paper-Scissor 3 times

    - The person who wins 2 goes first

    - If it's a tie, shoot again

2. Flip a coin

    - One person flips, the other calls H or T (Heads or Tails)

    - The flipper is the other side of the coin

    - Flip the coin one time

Ask students to explain what a "strategy" is? Now show the two basic strategies that can be used as a simple, fair way to determine who goes first when playing a game (or any other time really). Demonstrate how to play Rock-Paper-Scissor by having a student come up and showing. Be sure to explain the three combinations for winning (Rock beats Scissors, Scissors beat Paper, and Paper beats Rock). Also, explain that the partners must "shoot" at the same time. Next, demonstrate the coin flip using the steps above.

Practice

Guided Practice: Have two students come up to the front of the class and demonstrate the Rock-Paper-Scissor strategy. Have the class give them feedback to see if they did each step correctly. Now invite two more students to demonstrate the coin flip. Again, have the class give feedback and check that they included each step.

Perform

Independent Practice: Tell students that they will now get the opportunity to be teachers! Have students work individually or in small groups to design a poster showing the steps for one of the two strategies. Tell them they will be teaching this skill to a younger student in the school (or to a younger sibling, neighbor or friend). Have them create their poster and practice their teaching skills in small groups.

The Empower Program   **Lesson Plan 21**

Skill Set: Strive-Skills

Grade Range: K-2

Social Skill: Identifying Goals

Big Picture Goal: Development of self-motivation and activation skills.

Common Core Standard Link: CCSS.ELA-LITERACY.CCRA.SL.1

Materials: Talking piece (optional), paper, crayons

Objective: Students will be able to create a drawing, showing the skill steps for *Identifying Goals*, including a goal for themselves, using the skill card as a resource.

Hook

Create an experience: Ask your students if anyone has ever seen or played the game tag? Ask them what the point of the game is? When they tell you, write GOAL = *whatever they said* on the board. Now ask about other games like basketball or soccer. Write the same definition equation after.

Analyze the experience: Pass around a ball or "talking piece" and ask what they think the word GOAL means based on your discussion of those games? You can write Goal = _____ to make this more visual.

Teach

Define the skill: *How to set a goal for yourself.*

Identify the Skill Steps:

  1. Stop and think – What do I want to do?

  2. EYE-dentify with your eyes – Draw a picture of your goal

            What will it look like for you to get it?

  3. Give it words – Write or say, *"My goal is to _____"*

Start by defining what a goal is – something you want to achieve or get to. Use some examples from the beginning activity. Use physical gestures to cue *"Stop"* (hand out) and *"Think"* (pointing to your brain) and insert one of the example goals, *"What do I want to do? I want to _____."* For the second step, point to your eyes and teach them the "fancy" older kid word of *identify* and explain that this just means to see or point something out. Call on a volunteer to draw a picture of your example goal on the board or have a volunteer make the facial expression that they think they might have when they achieved that goal. Finally say, now let's give this picture words, *"My goal is to [insert goal]."*

Practice

Guided Practice: Write or show pictures of several different areas or places such as home, school, reading, math, sports, music, etc. As a group, brainstorm some things that students think they might want to be able to do in each of those areas. After a quick list of ideas is verbalized or written, have a student volunteer to go through all three steps of the social skill, ending in identifying a specific goal for one of the areas.

Perform

Independent Practice: Give each student paper and crayons and have them draw three boxes with arrows pointing in between each box consecutively like this BOX ⊠ BOX ⊠ BOX. Now have them choose a goal for themselves in any area they want and draw the three steps.

  1. A picture of what they want to do

  2. A picture of them achieving their goal

  3. Writing, *"My goal is to _____"*

The Empower Program   **Lesson Plan 22**

Skill Set: Strive-Skills

Grade Range: K-2

Social Skill: Breaking Down Big Goals

Big Picture Goal: Development of self-motivation and activation skills.

Common Core Standard Link: CCSS.ELA-LITERACY.CCRA.SL.1

Materials: Talking piece (optional), fake pizza ingredients (or pictures of), paper, crayons

Objective: Students will be able to create a pizza pie drawing showing the skill steps for *Breaking Down Big Goals* using the skill card as a resource.

Hook

Create an experience: Gather students around and explain that you will be making a pizza together. Ask them to brainstorm some steps that they might need to follow in order to make the pizza? Now follow those steps to make the pizza (either drawing it on the board or constructing it from paper props).

Analyze the experience: Pass around a ball or talking piece and analyze the experience of making the pizza. Ask students about their process. Did they just snap their fingers and a finished pizza magically appeared? Coax them to give feedback on how they broke it down and, more importantly, why they did so in the order they did.

Teach

Define the skill: *How to give your big goal little steps.*

Identify the Skill Steps:

  1. Stop and think – Pizza pie!

  2. Sort your ingredients – Draw the things that you think you need to make your goal

  3. Write your recipe – Make a list of 3 steps that you think you need to do to get to your goal

Review with students what a goal is. Now explain that sometimes a goal can seem too big to tackle all at once, but if we can break it into smaller steps, it becomes easy as (insert bad Italian accent here) "a pizza pie!" (insert cheesy wink here). Ask students what their "big goal" was in the beginning of this lesson by saying, *"Our goal was to make a _____ (pizza pie)."* For the first skill step, remind them that they have already broken a goal down into steps successfully as they made the pizza pie just now! SO have them echo with you, *"Stop and think – easy as pizza pie!"* For the second step, explain that they need to sort their ingredients for their goal, just like they did so for their pizza even though they won't be actual ingredients. For step three, tell students to *"write their recipe"* by making a small list of three simple steps they want to follow in order to get to or closer to their goal!

Practice

Guided Practice: Brainstorm goals that students have for various topics on the board using a visual web. Write GOALS in the bubble in the middle and invite students to come up and write (or you can) lines with new bubbles showing goals they have for school, home, etc. Now pick one by closing your eyes, spinning around and putting your hand on the board. Whichever goal bubble you are closest to will be the one for discussion! Ask students to use each skill step with you to break this big goal down into smaller steps.

Perform

Independent Practice: Have each student draw a circle on a piece of paper and write "Easy as pizza pie" on the top. Now have them cut the pie into 4 quadrants by drawing one line down the middle and one line across. Have them number their pieces 1-3 and then write each step into a piece. Tell them to leave the last piece empty because they will be using that to draw a picture of them achieving their goal! Give them time to work in pairs, groups or independently to complete their goal pies.

The Empower Program   Lesson Plan 23

Skill Set: Strive-Skills

Grade Range: K-2

Social Skill: Strategies to Reach Your Goals

Big Picture Goal: Development of self-motivation and activation skills.

Common Core Standard Link: CCSS.ELA-LITERACY.CCRA.SL.1

Materials: Talking piece (optional), index cards, paper, crayons

Objective: Students will be able to create a poster or staircase showing skill steps for *Strategies to Reach Your Goals* using the skill card as a resource.

Hook

Create an experience: Tell your students you will be playing a game of charades before you start this lesson, just for fun. Write on index cards or scraps of paper the following 6 words: Teacher, Baby, Pool, Bathroom (can change if you wish, but this is always funny), Pencil, and Hat. Now call a student up at a time (after reviewing the rules of charades) and have them act out the word. When the class guesses correctly, write the word on the board. Give a time limit to each actor (about 1 minute) and if they haven't guessed correctly, give the answer. Once all the words are written on the board begin to analyze.

Analyze the experience: Pass around a ball or talking piece and ask students if they can see anything that these words have in common (that's the same). Is there a way you can put them into groups? You are facilitating that students sort these words into PEOPLE, PLACES and THINGS.

Teach

Define the skill: *How to get to your goal.*

Identify the Skill Steps:

1. Stop and think – I need my nouns!

2. Choose your nouns:

   PERSON – *Who* can I use to help me?

   PLACE – *Where* is the best place?

   THINGS – *What* can I use to help me?

3. Ask your nouns for help:

   PEOPLE – Parents, Friends, Teachers, Coaches

   PLACE – Special place or special time

   THINGS – Timer, Post-it note, Divider, Chart

Use physical gestures to cue *"Stop"* (hand out) and *"Think"* (pointing to your brain) and then have students repeat after you, *"I need my nouns!"* Ask a student if anyone knows what a noun is? Explain that a noun is a person, place of thing. In order to get to our goals, we need to be very careful to choose only helpful nouns to be around us. Explain step two by having students echo each guiding question: *"Person - Who can I use to help me?" "PLACE - Where is the best place?" "THINGS - What can I use to help me?"* Explain that the second skill step is where we organize our nouns using these helpful questions! Finally introduce the final skill step by having students echo, *Ask my nouns for help!"*

Practice

Guided Practice: Have a student volunteer a goal or you can choose one to write on the board. Write or draw that goal at the top of the board. Now draw three lines leading up to that (like floating steps, you can also draw three steps like a staircase). Have students echo back the first skill step and list their noun groups aloud, *"People, places, things!"* Write step #1 on the first step on the board and write, *"I need my nouns!"* For the next step, write #2 on the line and ask students to choose a their nouns for this goal. Call on students to give a helpful person, place and thing that could help them with the goal at the top of the board. Use the guiding questions to help! Write these on the second step line. Now move to the third step, write #3 and ask students to model aloud how they would ask for these three helpful nouns? Use this as an opportunity to pull in other known social skills such as tone, face and body position!

Perform

Independent Practice: Give students a choice of which activity they would like to do to practice. The first choice is to make a poster where they draw and label helpful nouns in their life! The second choice is to create their own staircase, modeling the one you created on the board, for a goal of their own. Pass out necessary materials and give students time to work as you float around giving feedback and additional support.

The Empower Program   Lesson Plan 24
Skill Set: Strive-Skills
Grade Range: K-2

Social Skill: Strategies for Working in Groups

Big Picture Goal: Development of self-motivation and activation skills.
Common Core Standard Link: CCSS.ELA-LITERACY.CCRA.SL.1
Materials: Talking piece (optional), pictures or videos of sports teams, army, fire fighters, circus
Objective: Students will be able to work in a group to create a story while using skill steps for *Strategies for Working in Groups*, using the skill card as a resource, and providing feedback on use of steps.

Hook

Create an experience: Show student's pictures or even videos of the following groups of people: Army, Sports Teams, Firefighters, and Circus Performers (or any other combination of professional people working as a group together). Ask students what they think all of these different groups had in common, or did that was the same? You are trying to elicit they are all examples of adults whose jobs depend on them working together as a group to achieve a common goal!

Analyze the experience: Pass a ball or talking piece around and ask students to give other examples of adults or even kids who work in groups for a common goal? Write these on the board. Ask students if they noticed each person in the group had a different role and see if they can identify some different jobs each person did, even though they were working together for the same goal.

Teach

Define the skill: *How to work with others to get to your goal.*
Identify the Skill Steps:

1. Stop and think – What is our goal? (Write it so everyone can see)
2. Ask each other – What jobs can we each do well?
   - Write/Build/Draw (hands)
   - Listen (ears)
   - Organize (eyes)
   - Timer (mind)
3. Use a circle to work as a team!
   (Go in a circle as you work, giving each person a chance to do their job as you go around)

Use physical gestures to cue *"Stop"* (hand out) and *"Think"* (pointing to your brain) and have students echo, *"What is our goal?"* Ask students to think about the social skill of communication. Explain working in a group involves a lot of communication. Explain the second skill step involves asking the other people in your group what jobs they think they do well so you can all achieve your goal together. Have students identify the four key jobs for working in groups by mimicking your motions: HANDS (wave your hands in front) for writing, drawing or building, EARS (point to your ears) for listening, EYES (point to your eyes) for organizing and MIND (point to your brain) for keeping track of time. Introduce the last skill step by drawing a circle on the board and asking students to identify this shape. Explain we can use a circle to make sure everyone gets a chance to participate and do their job as we work together as a group!

Practice

Guided Practice: Invite four students who are showing excellent social skills (or have been that day) to use as models for guided practice. Drag their desks or a table to the front of the room. Explain the goal, as a group, is to create a story together about having a pet dinosaur and also present a poster. They will only have 5 minutes to do this. Now ask the rest of the class to guide them through the steps. For the first step, ask a class member to say the step aloud. Have a student in the model group write their goal on a piece of paper or post-it and place it in the middle of the table or of all of their desks. Ask the class for the second skill step. When they say it, allow the model group to attempt to divvy out the four jobs. If they run into problems choosing, offer the strategy of writing each job on a piece of paper and picking them out of a hat or from the table once they have been mixed up. Explain that the person who writes the steps on the pieces of paper is left with the last one. Once the model group has their jobs, ask the class for the last skill step. Ask the model group to demonstrate how to use a circle to go around and make sure everyone is doing their job. You can also use a concrete visual to help with the idea of moving in a circle such as passing the goal sheet around to each person in a circle as they do their job.

Use all interactions as moments to elicit feedback from the rest of the class to help solve problems as they come up. If no problems occur and students are doing well, elicit feedback explaining why the group is doing so well?

Perform

Independent Practice: Split the class into groups of four. If this doesn't work mathematically, explain that a student can do two jobs and again, elicit problem solving social skills previously learned if needed. Tell all groups they are to work on the same goal as the model group, after dispersing the model group members into different groups. Set a timer for 10 minutes and have the groups begin. Float around the room giving support and feedback.

The Empower Program   Lesson Plan 25
Skill Set: Strive-Skills
Grade Range: K-2

Social Skill: Finding Focus

Big Picture Goal: Development of self-motivation and activation skills.
Common Core Standard Link: CCSS.ELA-LITERACY.CCRA.SL.1
Materials: Talking piece (optional), ball
Objective: Students will be able to perform skill steps of *Finding Focus* with a partner using the skill card as a resource.

Hook

Create an experience: Ask a student to come to the front of the room and help you understand how to do the latest dance or play the latest video game. As they are explaining the steps, become immediately and visibly distracted by starting to itch the bottom of your foot. Then apologize and say, *"Sorry what were you saying again?"* As the student begins talking again, let your eyes trail off them to the corner of the room and begin staring and say, *"Did you see that shadow on the wall! It looked like a giraffe!"* Hopefully the student gives you an annoyed look to which you again reply, *"Sorry, you were saying . . . "* As soon as they begin, turn around and say, *"Did you hear that? I think I heard a siren . . . "* Then apologize again and allow the student to continue. Finally, look sad and start looking down at your feet again. If the student asks you to look up or asks what's wrong say, *"I just keep thinking about my favorite pencil that I lost yesterday. I wonder where it is . . . "*

Analyze the experience: Pass a ball or talking piece around and ask students for feedback on your behavior as the listener. Write some of their ideas on the board. Say sometimes it can be really hard to focus when there are so many ways you can become distracted. Ask for a show of hands if anyone can relate. Now explain you will be learning a social skill today that can help to identify how you are being distracted and help you find your focus again!

Teach

Define the skill: *How to find your focus when you are distracted.*

Identify the Skill Steps:

1. Stop and think – Where in my body am I feeling distracted?
2. Use a song to find out where – *"Head . . . Shoulders, Eyes or Ears!"*
   Head – A worry?
   Shoulders – A body feeling?
   Eyes – A thing you can see?
   Ears – A sound?
3. Tell someone, *"I feel distracted by _____"*

Use physical gestures to cue *"Stop"* (hand out) and *"Think"* (pointing to your brain) and have students echo, *"Where in my body am I feeling distracted?"* For the next skill step, ask students if they have ever heard the song "Head, shoulders, knees and toes"? Sing the melody of the song, but change the words to, *"Head . . . Shoulders, Eyes and Ears, Eyes and Ears!"* Have students point to each body part as they sing, like the original song. Go through this several times, getting faster each time for fun! Now explain each of these parts of our body can help to tell us a way that we might be feeling distracted. Point to head and have students do the same while repeating, *"A worry?"* Point to shoulders and have students repeat, *"A body feeling?"* Point to eyes and have students repeat, *"Something you can see?"* Point to ears and have students repeat, *"A sound?"* Now tell students the final skill step is to ask someone for help by telling him or her what is distracting you! Model how to do this by asking a student to be the teacher. Switch places and sit in their desk or on their spot on the rug and have them call on you. Say, *"Ms. or Mr. _____, that sound outside is distracting me. Can you help?"*

Practice

Guided Practice: Explain we are now going to practice identifying some different ways we can all be distracted as a class so when these come up, we can remember to ask for help! Tell students since they are now social skills all-stars, you would like to introduce them to Speed Ball! Explain they will all sit in a circle. You will set a timer for 2 minutes and give a challenge. Then they will work as a team to come up with as many answers to that challenge as they can by putting their hands up and passing the ball to each other to call out the answers. You, the teacher, will then write these answers on the board as fast as you can! For the first challenge ask the group, *"Name worries you might have during the school day . . . ready . . . GO!"* For the second challenge ask, *"Name feelings in your body that could be distracting?"* For the third challenge ask, *"Name things you can see that might be distracting?"* For the final challenge ask, *"Name things you might hear that could be distracting?"* For fun, count the students total score as a team and do a happy dance to celebrate the many AWESOME ideas!

Perform

Independent Practice: Have students break into pairs and go over the skill steps with each other. Have one student start as the student and the other student act as the helper if they forget a part of a step. Students switch. This can be short, but give students a chance to go through the motions of using each step independently.

APPENDIX C

MOTIVATION P.O.P RESOURCES

Quick Guide to Student Access Supports

Supporting Students with Extra Energy/Easily Distracted	Supporting Students with Content Access	Supporting Students with Executive Functioning/Organization
❑ Provide a "fidget" to squeeze while they listen or work (sand ball, silly putty, bean bag, play-doh, felt ball, etc.) ❑ Give option to move within lesson for helpful reason (passing out papers, collecting materials, sorting materials, helping to hold book for read aloud, walking back and forth to office, etc.) ❑ Make sure to include options for VAKT as much as possible within lessons: **(V)isual** - use pictures, allow student to draw picture of content, multi-media, color-coding, **(A)uditory** – allow students to listen to books on tape, speech-to-text options, use sounds to highlight content (such as clapping syllables), use music as base for memorization (insert content points into a song or rap) **(K)inesthetic** – use movement to enhance content (clapping, jumping, acting out, using gross-motor movements, out of seat options such as laying on rug on belly or sitting on imaginary chair aka squatting, throwing a ball or object for question/answers) **(T)actile** – using physically stimulating materials to enhance teaching such as play-doh, shampoo in a ziplock bag to trace letters, sand, textured cloth, silly putty, soft fabric, feathers, etc.	❑ Provide manipulatives to make content concrete and visual (blocks, counters, chips, colored markers, etc.) ❑ Give examples (connected to a known topic/skill set) ❑ Use Graphic Organizers ❑ Use Text-Speech App ❑ Audio Books to listen as they read/look at the words ❑ Use a peer tutor to help ❑ Be sure content is at child's actual readiness level (if that is significantly lower than grade level, provide review material at their remedial level to increase confidence prior to bridging to grade level) ❑ Give more 1-1 attention if possible with a teacher or small group ❑ Provide an outline or key points before lesson ❑ Provide a diagram when needed before lesson, then ask students to physically point to the diagram to orient them to lesson content as you go ❑ Break down the prior-knowledge skills necessary to tackle new learning and provide review lesson for student prior to new instruction ❑ Connect content to subject matter or topic student is highly motivated by (even if not at all connected to learning content) ❑ Use humor to relax student and provide access to content in funny way (inserting new learning into knock-knock jokes that they can re-tell, for instance)	❑ Use visual checklists ❑ Color-Code folders with work, tasks, necessary steps ❑ Use bins, bags, containers to separate and give a specific landing place for all materials, assignments etc. ❑ Give students a daily planner (schedule, list of activities, checklist for times of day that go by, area to write down HW or behavioral expectations that are needed for each chunk of their day) ❑ Use colored paper to block off portions of page or reading to be less overwhelming and break up work ❑ Use colored highlighters to chunk work into smaller parts (having student check off each block they have completed) OR physically cut page into smaller sections to break up work so it becomes more like a game than a sheet of paper with work on it. ❑ Help student build and use a binder ❑ Use timers or countdown clocks during independent work to orient the student towards time use and staying on task ❑ Give frequent time checks (10 more minutes, 5 more minutes, 1 more minute…etc.) ❑ Use post-it notes to show small chunks of content. Then move those notes around as you discuss or practice content allowing student to interact and organize the information in new ways without having to remember it.

Name: _____

Date: _____

My Simple Tracker

My goal for today is...	(Insert social skill card here)

My goal for today is...

_____

- -

_____

- -

_____

- -

⬇ A picture of my goal ⬇

SKILL STEPS   **VISUALS**

Watch me SHOW what I KNOW!

Name: _____

Date: _____

My Schedule Tracker

My Goal:	A picture of my goal

My Goal:

_____

- -

_____

A picture of my goal

My Schedule | My Color Scale

When the clock looks like...	Time	Class Activity	G	Y	R
(clock)			○	○	○
(clock)			○	○	○
(clock)			○	○	○
(clock)			○	○	○
(clock)			○	○	○
(clock)			○	○	○
(clock)			○	○	○

HELPING SPACE

I can use ⬇ social skill to help me:

SKILL STEPS	VISUALS

JUST IN CASE...

If I need help I can:

_____

_____

If I get upset I can:

_____

_____

HOW DID I DO?

I earned _____ GREEN's today.

I earned _____ YELLOW's today.

I earned _____ RED's today.

_____
My Name

_____
My Teachers Name

Name: _____

Date: _____

My GOAL → REWARD Tracker

GOALS

My goal today is to   (this looks like...)

(GREEN)
_____

- -

_____

I will work on   (this looks like...)

(YELLOW)
_____

- -

_____

I will NOT   (this looks like...)

(RED)
_____

- -

_____

REWARD

By SHOWING my goal behavior, I am working to earn:

(Me showing my goal behavior)   →   (Me earning my reward)

I can use the tracker on the back to keep track of my choices! ➡

MY GOAL TRACKER

My GREEN choices today	My YELLOW choices today	My RED choices today

HOW DID I DO?

GREEN's	YELLOW's	RED's
_____	_____	_____

Did I earn my reward?   YES   NO

Why?

_____   _____
My Name   My Teachers Name

About the Author

Rachel Baker has worked in public, residential, and charter schools as an inclusive education teacher, social worker, and director of special education for 10 years. She earned her Bachelor's degree in Elementary Education and Special Education from La Salle University and her Master's degree in social work from the University of Pennsylvania's School of Social Policy and Practice, with an emphasis on social justice, and education equity. After receiving her MSW, she returned to the classroom to bridge her experience as an educator with her advocacy for the prioritization of social–emotional learning.

She implemented the first phases of *The Empower Program* in both public and private elementary and middle school settings. She has spoken at several national and local conferences including the NAEYC National Conference and Expo and the ASAH Annual Conference and provided professional development for schools and after-school programs. She currently facilitates a youth group in Camden, New Jersey, where middle school boys meet weekly to discuss their role as leaders in the community.

Additionally, she works with individual students and families as an outpatient therapist for the Child Guidance Resource Center in Philadelphia where she utilizes The Empower Program to provide concrete social skills instruction and strategies through individual and family-based therapy. She also works for Montclair State University mentoring in-service teachers in the P-3 Alternate Route Teaching Program.

Her ultimate goal is to use *The Empower Program* to operationalize positive behavioral support and culturally responsive climate for all students in all schools, especially those in less equitable socio-economic settings.